cathy cassidy

Letters to Cathy

PUFFIN

Books by Cathy Cassidy

For older readers
DIZZY
DRIFTWOOD
INDIGO BLUE
SCARLETT
SUNDAE GIRL
LUCKY STAR
GINGERSNAPS
ANGEL CAKE

DREAMS AND DOODLES DAYBOOK

For younger readers
SHINE ON, DAIZY STAR

PUFFIN BOOKS

Published by the Penguin Group: London, New York, Australia, Canada,
India, Ireland, New Zealand and South Africa
Penguin Books Ltd, Registered Offices: 80 Strand, London WC2R 0RL, England
puffinbooks.com

First published 2009
2

Set in Century Gothic Regular
Made and printed in England by Clays Ltd, St Ives plc

British Library Cataloguing in Publication Data
A CIP catalogue record for this book is available from the British Library

ISBN: 978–0–141–32894–2

www.greenpenguin.co.uk

Mixed Sources
Product group from well-managed
forests and other controlled sources
www.fsc.org Cert no. SA-COC-1592
© 1996 Forest Stewardship Council
FSC

Penguin Books is committed to a sustainable future
for our business, our readers and our planet.
The book in your hands is made from paper
certified by the Forest Stewardship Council.

To my readers . . .
This one's for you!

Contents

1. Friends Forever? 1

Making Friends / Keeping Friends / Falling Out

2. Growing Up 23

Body Matters / Girl Talk / Skin Deep / Mixed-Up
Feelings

3. Boys, Boys, Boys 42

First Crush / Taking Your Time / Love Hurts /
Breaking Up

4. School Daze 59

School's Cool! / Teacher's Pet? / Teacher Trouble / Work
It Out / School Blues

5. Beat Bullying 83

Don't Pick On Me / Sticks and Stones / Speaking Out /
An End to Bullying

6. Confidence Tricks 106

Accept Yourself / Making Friends With You / Look for the
Good Stuff! / Get Happy! / Do it Anyway! / Get Lucky!

7. Being Yourself 126

Who Am I? / Style Matters / Let It Out / Peer Pressure /
Role Models / Being Different / No Such Thing as Perfect

8. Dream On 149

Big Ideas / Fame at Last / Making It Happen

9. Family Matters 163

Super Strict? / Brothers and Sisters / Problem Parents . . .
/ . . . and Parent Problems! / Patchwork Families

10. Sad Stuff 182

Bereavement / When Someone is Ill / Scary Stuff /
Broken Families

11. Things That Don't Help 203

Don't Worry! / Little White Lies / Self-destruct / Rebel
Rebel / Looking for Love? / Hurting Inside / Food Wars /
Running Away

12. . . . and Things That Do! 230

Negotiate! / Talk It Over / Expert Help / Feeling Understood / Express Yourself! / Get Moving! / Believe It or
Not . . . / Back to Nature / Good Stuff! / The Fab Five

1. Friends Forever?

Friendship is one of the most important things in our lives. It's the glue that sticks us together through good times and bad. A real friend will be there for you through the best and the worst of times, loyal, caring, thoughtful, fun. Good friends are a little like family, and a best friend can often be the person who knows and understands you best in the world.

So, are friends forever?

Well, sometimes. At this stage in your life, you're growing up, changing, working out who you really are . . . and sometimes, that means outgrowing old friends. It can take luck, hard work and effort on both sides to keep a friendship strong. And sometimes, no matter what you do, things fall apart . . .

Making Friends

Dear Cathy
My friends all went to different
secondary schools and I'm
struggling to make friends.

I need help fast!
Tammi, age 11

Cathy
I'm going to be moving to a new high
school in the middle of the term, miles
away from my old school and friends.
I'm dreading it. Everyone will know
each other and I know I'll never
fit in . . .
Sumayya, age 13

To make new friends, you have to be friendly!
You have to take a risk, make an effort, try talking
to people you may not know very well. Smile, chat,
ask questions, give compliments, listen, support
. . . and make it a part of who you are. You'll soon
make new contacts, and slowly, from there, new
friendships may develop.

If, like Tammi, you're struggling, try mixing
things up a little. Rather than rely on her classmates,
Tammi could look further afield – join lunchtime
clubs or after-school groups. She should choose a
club or group that interests her – drama, art, sport,
athletics, dance, debating, maths, music, whatever.

That way, she'll be meeting people she already has something in common with. Working on something together, whether it's a play, a concert or a netball match, brings people together and breaks the ice.

Tammi wants some close friends, but true friendship takes time to develop. She needs to be patient . . . those new friends are out there!

Starting a new school mid-term, like Sumayya, is not easy, but it can be a great way to meet new mates! She may not enjoy being the centre of attention, but her new classmates will be curious and interested, and most will want to make her welcome. Sumayya will have to take a deep breath and make sure she sees the change of school as an opportunity to make new friends, not a disaster that is ruining her life. She may not have chosen this, but it's happening – and her best option is to accept that and make the most of it.

So, how do you make new mates? For some people it's easy, for others a nightmare, but one thing's for sure – if you're feeling lonely, you need to get out there and make some new connections.

Why do some people collect new mates the way the rest of us collect zits and split ends? Watch those people and you'll see that they have skills that literally attract others to them!

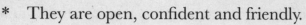

* They are open, confident and friendly.
* They smile!
* They are kind, supportive and generous.
* They are genuinely interested in others.
* They take time to chat about anything and everything.
* They give and receive compliments easily.
* They remember names and details.
* They are enthusiastic!
* They are upbeat, positive and fun to be around.
* They are interesting . . . They have things to talk about!
* They are not afraid to make plans . . . and include others in them.

Maybe those are qualities we could all work on having!

Keeping Friends ❀❀❀❀❀❀❀

Hey Cathy
My best buddy has moved away and although I have other friends, it's just not the same. I cry myself to sleep sometimes because I miss her so much.

Lissi, age 10

Dear Cathy
Last month I moved to Spain with my family. I'm settling in better than I thought, but I've noticed that already my old friends don't write, ring or email as often as they used to. I don't want them to forget me! What can I do?

Karis, age 12

Being separated from good friends is hard, as Lissi and Karis have discovered. Nobody wants to lose touch, but long-distance friendship can be a challenge.

Both Lissi and Karis need to keep the lines of communication open with texts, emails, messaging, letters and phone calls. Make plans to visit or meet up in the future, so you have something to look forward to and talk about. Websites like Bebo and Piczo are good ways to stay in touch with distant friends, as you can post pictures too!

Lissi is feeling left behind and lonely, but turning back the clock is not an option. She needs to focus on her remaining friends, arranging cool days out, sleepovers and fun times, making an effort to move on and start enjoying life again.

Karis is feeling hurt that her old friends aren't in touch as regularly as they once were. Again, the way forward is to get more involved in her new life – worrying about her old friends will stop her from moving forward and giving new friendships a fair chance.

Both of my two best friends live hundreds of miles away from me, yet we've managed to keep the friendships strong. A good friendship can survive separation, especially if both of you are determined to stay close, but some friendships will fade. Don't beat yourself up about this. Hang on to the happy memories and move forward – the world is full of friends you haven't met yet.

Cathy

Please help me. I have just had an argument with my friend - she said that I wasn't pretty enough to get a boyfriend, and this really upset me. It feels like she's just trying to hurt me and I don't know why!

Fiona, age 11

Jealousy isn't called the green-eyed monster for nothing! Don't let it mess your friendship up. Fiona's friend is almost certainly feeling insecure – she's lashing out at Fiona to make herself feel better. Not a great plan, obviously! Fiona needs to be honest and let her friend know how hurtful this comment was.

It can feel scary to confront a friend when you're feeling upset, so think out what you want to say first. Stick to talking about how you felt and avoid accusations – that won't help, and could make things a whole lot worse. Let your friend know you need her support and, hopefully, you can come through this kind of straight-talking chat feeling closer than ever.

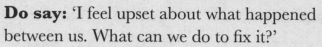

Do say: 'I feel upset about what happened between us. What can we do to fix it?'

Don't say: 'I'll never forgive you for treating me this way!'

Do say: 'I'd like to understand more about why you said what you did. Can you explain what made you feel that way?'

Don't say: 'Why are you being so bitchy?'

Do say: 'How can we make our friendship stronger?'

Don't say: 'I'm so sick of you! Forget it!'

Hi Cathy

My best friend is great at a lot of things like dance, drama and singing, but there's nothing very special about me. I feel really dull and boring, like I'll always be in her shadow.

Nina, age 12

Nina is letting envy poison her friendship, and that's seriously bad news. Part of her jealousy stems from lack of self-esteem – she doesn't see her own cool, unique qualities because she's so busy feeling envious of her friend! Nina feels outclassed, but friendship is not a competition . . . real friends admire and support each other's talents and good qualities. Nina has to start rating her own good points and learn to feel happy about them . . . then she won't feel so threatened by her friend's talents.

Dear Cathy
My friend Shanie has got in with a bad crowd. She doesn't seem to bother about school any more, and she's started smoking. She says it's no big deal. I'm really worried about her.

Hasmita, age 12

Dear Cathy
My mum doesn't approve of my best friend and hates me hanging out with her. My bezzie can be a rebel, but she's a great friend and is always there for me. I wish my mum could just see that.

Leanne, age 14

Sometimes, a friend seems to go right off the rails. Hasmita is right to be concerned – a sudden change of character can signal problems at home. She could try letting Shanie know she's worried – if there is something more behind this, Shanie may just find the courage to open up about it. Often, an attempt to help a friend who is heading for trouble can meet with a brick wall, but that doesn't mean you shouldn't at least try – it shows your friend you care about her, and that's important. If that happens here, all Hasmita can do is step back – and be there as a friend if and when Shanie needs her in the future.

Leanne's mum may seem disapproving, but her concern, like Hasmita's, stems from worry. She sees Leanne's friend as a bad influence, someone who may drag her down, wreck her life, mess up her school record, lead her into all kinds of trouble.

Leanne needs to realize that her mum loves her and is trying to protect her, but also knows that her friend is loyal and supportive. She should talk to her mum about this and encourage her to get to know this girl properly. Leanne may not totally change her mum's mind, but talking things through can only help.

Falling Out

Cathy

I've just had a mega fight with my
friends, and the worst thing is I know I
was at least partly to blame. They're not
speaking to me now and I'm scared I've
lost them for good!

Maxine, age 13

Dear Cathy

I was upset yesterday over
something that happened at home
and I took it out on my best friend.
I know I've really hurt her feelings
and I really regret being mean.
Now she's gone off with someone
else and everyone is blaming me . . .

Karina, age 11

We've all made mistakes, like Maxine and Karina
. . . the trick is to learn from them. If you're in the
wrong, swallow your pride and apologize. It can

take a while for friends to forgive you or learn to trust you again after a split, but if you show how much you regret what happened, most will give you another chance.

I had a big fallout with school friends when I was fourteen, and I was to blame . . . I'd been jealous of a new girl who joined our group and said some mean things about her behind her back. The group let me know I was out of order . . . and for a few days I was left to think about what I'd done, alone and friendless.

In the end, too ashamed to face my friends, I wrote a letter of apology explaining just how much I regretted my words. I tried to let them know I'd lashed out from feelings of insecurity rather than just plain malice, and made an effort to put things right with the girl I'd bitched about too. My friends accepted me back into the group, but I was really shaken by the whole experience. It made me think very hard about the way I'd acted.

Did I want to be a mean girl, someone who talked about people behind their backs? No way. People judge you by the way you act and the things you say – they don't look too hard at whether you're lashing out because you're scared, worried, insecure or jealous. Always put yourself in the other person's shoes and imagine how you'd feel to be on the receiving end of that kind of thing . . . and if you wouldn't like it, don't do it.

Dear Cathy
My best friend can be so embarrassing! She's not really into fashion or music and she has zero interest in boys - she's only interested in kittens and Beanie toys. Some of the kids in my year think she's weird. I just wish she could grow up a bit . . .

Pippa, age 12

Please help, Cathy!
My best friend is starting to really bug me. I had my hair cut a few weeks ago, and the next weekend she had hers styled exactly like it. Then she bought the same Rocket Dog pumps as me and even the same kind of

ruffled skirt I wear for school. Why does she have to copy everything I do?

Ellie, age 14

Friends are rarely perfect . . . we're not, so why should they be? Pippa is worried about how others see her friend, and wishes she would grow up a little faster. I suspect Pippa's friend is quite happy just being herself and really isn't worried about 'fitting in'. It can be tricky when you grow up at different rates and suddenly find yourselves with very different interests and ideas. This can pull a friendship apart. Friendships change and evolve as we grow up, but being different can be cool! To keep the friendship strong, Pippa needs to stop feeling embarrassed by her friend and accept her for who she is.

Ellie's friend is trying a little *too* hard to fit in. Imitation is supposed to be flattering, but as Ellie has discovered, it can be pretty annoying too. Instead of getting wound up by the whole thing, she can turn the situation around by offering to give her friend a new, unique look that's perfect for her. The two can go shopping together and pick out styles that are cool, but different . . . sorted!

Hello Cathy
Last week, my friend Jade came to my house for tea and we had a nice time. On Monday morning, for no reason I can think of, she started spreading nasty rumours about me and my family all around the school. I'm so hurt! I tried to talk to her about it, but she says I'm taking it all too seriously. How much more serious can it be?

Zoe, age 10

Dear Cathy
I really identify with your book *GingerSnaps*. My best friend is exactly like Shannon. She uses people, and only likes me when I agree to go along with everything she says. I'm not sure if I even want a friend like this - it's so one-sided!

Marisa, age 13

With friends like this, who needs enemies? Zoe's friend Jade is a user. She enjoyed Zoe's hospitality, then turned it against her by spreading nasty gossip about her and her family. Zoe says she can't think of a reason Jade would do this. Perhaps Jade is having problems at home, or struggling with problems of her own – lashing out may help her to feel better about herself, however briefly. Sometimes, though, girls like Jade don't need a reason – they just like the attention gossip can bring them. Luckily, people will see this – many will sympathize with Zoe and be wary of Jade as a result.

It hurts, yes, but the truth is that some girls do not make good mates. They have a mean, poisonous streak that will sabotage any attempt at lasting friendship, and if there have been other instances where Jade has treated Zoe badly, perhaps it's time for Zoe to see this and let go of this relationship.

Marisa is starting to work out that her friendship too is not what it seems. If you act like a doormat, don't be too surprised if people wipe their feet on you! Marisa needs to change the rules in this friendship and make it clear she is not a pushover, and that may not go down too well with her friend!

Once you stop being a doormat, you start asking all kinds of questions . . . and Marisa is clearly in the process of working out whether this friendship is one she wants to continue with. It may be worth her talking honestly to her friend about how she'd like things to be more equal.

Some friends are bad for us. They're the ones who try to change us, who want us to do things we don't want to do. Perhaps they put us down the whole time, or make us feel bad with their negative moans or bitchy gossip. Friends who play games with our feelings are especially toxic. A bad friendship can destroy your self-esteem and mess with your head. Don't stay in a friendship that is getting you down. Step back, put a little space between you and look around for some better friends.

If you'd like to give a flagging friendship one last chance, though, by all means give it a go. If a heart-to-heart isn't helping to patch things up, ask your teacher for some help to sort out the problems and smooth things over. Most things can be fixed if you both want to fix them – and with effort on both sides, the most unlikely friendships can be rescued!

Help!
A while back I fell out – big style – with my best mate. We've been working on it and we've made up, but our friendship is still shaky. I don't want to lose her, but things just don't feel the same.

Molly, age 13

Dear Cathy

My friends have started to leave me
out of things. Sometimes they do stuff
and don't invite me, and some days they
don't even let me hang out with them
at break. They always have excuses, but
I know I'm losing them and it makes
me feel so sad!

Kirstin, age 10

Friendships are not always forever. Maybe there's a row or a falling-out, as happened with Molly, or maybe it's more of a slow drifting apart, as is happening with Kirstin. Either way, it hurts!

Molly can see that although her friendship has been patched up, there are still cracks in it – cracks that could one day break things apart for good. She can prepare herself for this by stepping back from the friendship a little and getting to know new groups of people. Once things don't feel quite so intense, Molly may even find a way to keep this friendship ticking over . . . even if it's no longer quite at best-friends level.

Kirstin is in a tougher situation. She wants to stay close to her friends, but finds herself constantly isolated and pushed aside. This is chipping away at her confidence and making her miserable . . . not good. Kirstin's friends have already moved on – they're just not honest enough to come right out and admit it. Kirstin needs to look around for new mates who will treat her with more respect.

Friendship is always a work in progress . . . it changes all the time, because we are changing too. You can never have too many friends! Don't expect one friend to fill all of your needs – that's a pretty tall order. If your best friend lets you down, what then? It's great to have a best friend, one special person who ticks all the boxes, who knows you inside out, but as you get older you will almost certainly find you are broadening your friendship base and making new mates. That's great!

I have two best friends and a whole bunch of others . . . some are great for hugs, advice and heart-to-hearts; some for wild times, festivals, adventures, laughs; some for girly nights in with a slushy DVD and a slab of chocolate cake. All of those things are important!

Make sure your friends know you appreciate them . . . and remember to be a great friend to others. It works both ways!

Helpbox

Read It . . .

* *Think Pink* by Lisa Clark (Macmillan)
* *Best of Friends* by Sophie Parkin (Piccadilly)
* *Chicken Soup for the Teenage Soul: The Real Deal* by Jack Canfield and Mark Hansen (Health Communications)

Websites:

www.childline.org.uk – sections on friendship; helping a friend; peer pressure
www.cathycassidy.com – click the Friendship Charter link and sign up to keep these six simple promises to make sure your friendship stays strong!

THE FRIENDSHIP CHARTER: 6 EASY STEPS TO MAKING A DIFFERENCE

1

I promise to show — and tell — my friends how much they mean to me. Often!

2

I promise to always listen and be there for my friends . . . through thick and thin.

3

I promise to hug the people I care about and take time out to have fun with them!

4

I promise never to knowingly hurt a friend.

5

I promise to do one random act of kindness every day (even if it's just the washing up!).

6

I promise to speak out if I see someone being bullied — and make an effort to be friendly to the victim too.

Check *cathycassidy.com* for details of the next *My Best Friend Rocks* Competition . . . a perfect way to show a special friend how much he/she means to you. You could even win the sleepover of your dreams!

On the website, you can also find out more about *National Best Friends' Day* . . . and how to celebrate it! What are you waiting for?

Cathy's Books . . . Published by Puffin

* *Shine on, Daizy Star* (jealousy, lies, being honest with friends)
* *GingerSnaps* (being yourself in a friendship, making choices about whether a friendship is good for you)
* *Indigo Blue* (jealousy, coping when a friend goes cool on you)
* *Driftwood* (helping a friend in trouble)
* *Sundae Girl* (learning to let friends get close to you)
* *Dizzy* (when friendship has to take the place of family)
* *Lucky Star* (new friendships and old, trust, loyalty)
* *Angel Cake* (making new friends from scratch)
* *Scarlett* (good friends and bad, and how to tell the difference . . .)

2. Growing Up

Just when you think you've got life sussed, the whole growing-up thing sneaks up on you and turns everything upside down. It's called puberty, and it's majorly weird!

What's puberty? At school, they'll tell you it's all about becoming a woman . . . but who wants to be a woman at the age of nine? Or twelve? Or fourteen, even? It sounds kind of scary. You just want to be YOU. Nature has other ideas, though, and suddenly your body is playing all kinds of crazy tricks on you . . .

Boobs. Periods. Spots. And mood swings that can have you laughing one minute, raging the next, and sobbing into your pillow a moment later. Help!!!

Body Matters ❀ ❀ ❀ ❀ ❀ ❀ ❀

Dear Cathy

I'm so unhappy. I am nine years old and already I have to wear a bra. The boys at school make comments and try to ping my bra strap through my shirt, and even my friends think I'm a freak. What can I do?

Tina, age 9

☆ 23 ☆

Hiya, Cathy

All of my friends have got really good
figures, but I'm pancake-flat. Seriously,
I look like a boy. I've started wearing
a padded bra because I'm sick of the
comments, but everyone knows I
don't need one at all. Will I ever start
to develop?

Elaine, age 13

Ouch. It can be tough to be the first one in your class
to hit puberty – and just as tough to be the last!

Tina is really shy about her new shape – after
all, it's a lot to get used to at the age of nine! The
boys who tease her probably don't mean any
harm – they may just be curious – but their jokes
make Tina more self-conscious than ever, and if
left unchecked this could turn into harassment or
bullying. Tina needs to talk to her teacher about
this, so that the boys back off.

Tina isn't getting the support she needs from
her friends, either . . . though I bet most of them
are quite envious of her. Tina needs to accept
her new body, because the more she shows her
embarrassment and unhappiness, the more likely
she is to be teased. This is a situation where acting

cool and confident, even though you might not feel it, is the answer.

Pretty soon, Tina's friends will be asking her for advice on bras and boobs and growing-up stuff, and the boys will be too in awe of her to dare ping her bra strap.

Elaine has given up hope of ever developing curves, and that's just as hard as being an early developer! The truth is, though, that puberty can hit at almost any time between nine and fifteen. What's normal for one girl will be totally different for another – we all have our own body clock, our own rate of development. And that's OK – growing up is not a race.

Elaine too needs to relax and try not to worry . . . those curves are coming, and soon!

Dear Cathy
My friends say they envy my boobs, but I hate them! They're just too big and I feel really shy and awkward about them. I hate the summer because it's too hot to wear a sweatshirt and everyone can see my bra through my white shirt.
Amaal, age 13

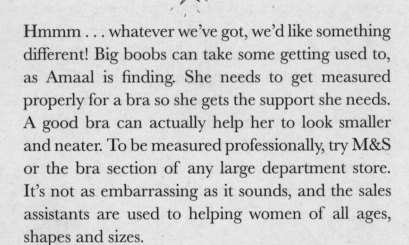

Cathy

I have really small boobs and I'd love to be a bit bigger. I don't think it's going to happen, as my mum is pretty small as well. I'll never get a boyfriend at this rate.

Gemma, age 15

Hmmm . . . whatever we've got, we'd like something different! Big boobs can take some getting used to, as Amaal is finding. She needs to get measured properly for a bra so she gets the support she needs. A good bra can actually help her to look smaller and neater. To be measured professionally, try M&S or the bra section of any large department store. It's not as embarrassing as it sounds, and the sales assistants are used to helping women of all ages, shapes and sizes.

See-through white school shirts in summer are a problem for all girls, big or small. Try wearing a plain, pretty vest underneath to spare the blushes.

Gemma too needs to accept that she's a slinky, skinny shape – and try to be glad about it! The top catwalk models share her slim proportions, and like them, she'll look good in almost any style. As for boys, for most of them, a pretty face and a fun personality count for a whole lot more than bra size – I promise.

Girl Talk

Hi Cathy
I'm think that my periods could start soon, but I don't know how to tell my mum or ask her about pads ... and I'd never have the courage to buy my own. How can I make sure I'm ready?

Charlie, age 12

Cathy
I really need a bra, but I don't have the money to buy one for myself and I'm way too shy to ask my mum. She thinks I'm still six years old!

Eilidh, age 11

The thing about mums is that they were kids once too. They've been through all this puberty stuff themselves! They won't be shocked or embarrassed or horrified. OK, some mums may not realize you're growing up so fast, but let them know and they'll be there for you.

Breaking the ice can be hard if you're not used to talking about personal stuff with your mum, but choose a time when you're alone together, take a deep breath . . . and do it. Once you've got things out in the open, your mum will take it from there. Growing up is a tricky time, and it really helps if you have someone you can talk it through with . . . a sympathetic mum is ideal, but if that's not possible, confiding in a big sister/ cousin/aunt can be a lifesaver.

Buying a bra – especially a first bra – is important. It's best to get measured properly and be sure you have the right size, and Eilidh's mum can arrange this and advise her. Charlie needs to tell her mum that she's getting ready for her periods too, but buying pads doesn't have to be a hassle. She can always tag along on the next supermarket trip and put a packet into the trolley . . . easy!

Help!
Some of my friends have started their

periods, and I know I need to think about it too. Should I use pads or tampons? And what if I start while I'm at school? I'd die of shame!

Sarah, age 12

Dear Cathy
I love swimming and go to a training club three times a week. My best friend says you can't swim when you have your period — is this true?

Annika, age 11

Sarah and Annika are right to plan out how they'll cope when their periods start . . . it makes sense to know what to expect. Sarah should gather as much info as she can and carry a wrapped pad in a secret pocket of her school bag just in case of emergencies.

Many girls worry about starting their period at school, or while at a friend's house, perhaps, but there's no need to stress out — a first period is often just a smudge rather than a flood. First period or not, if you do start unexpectedly at school, go along to the office and let them know, or confide in your form tutor — all schools have a supply of emergency pads for pupils in just this situation.

One girl I know started her periods while staying overnight at a friend's house . . . the first she knew about it was a faint smudge of red on the sheet. She was horrified, but she asked for help, and the friend's mum took the situation in her stride, changing the sheet and sorting her out with clean undies and a pad. Remember, never be scared to ask for help – us females are in this together!

The decision on whether to use pads or tampons is a personal one, but pads are often simpler to begin with. Annika need not worry about missing out on swimming, though – periods are a natural part of life, and it's fine to carry on with your favourite sport, no matter what time of the month it is. If you want to swim, however, you must use tampons because pads, which are worn outside the body, will disintegrate in water. Not good!!!

Some girls find tampons take a little getting used to at first, but once you've sussed them they are discreet, secure and very reliable . . . and if you want to, you can use them right from your very first period.

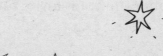

Hi Cathy

Sometimes I get period pains. A hot water bottle helps, but is there anything else I can do?

Lizzi, age 13

Not everybody gets period cramps, but some, like Lizzi, do. It's no fun, but you don't have to put up with it – there are lots of things you can try. Many girls find that gentle exercise relaxes the cramping muscles and eases the pain . . . so if Lizzi is at school, she shouldn't skive off games! If she's at home, some gentle yoga stretches, a bike ride or just dancing around for a while really can make a difference. OK, you may not feel like exercising, but give it a go . . . it helps.

If the cramps persist, Lizzi could try massaging her tummy, sipping hot drinks or taking a warm, relaxing bath. Still no change? Time to try painkillers – a chemist can suggest over-the-counter painkillers specially formulated for period pain, but if cramps are really severe, Lizzi should see her doctor for advice.

Skin Deep

Cathy

My skin gets really spotty just
before period time, and my hair
seems to be greasier too . . . it
really bugs me!

Chloe, age 12

Hi Cathy

I know everyone gets teenage spots,
but mine are beyond a joke – they're
really angry and red and sore. It's
not like I eat loads of chocolate or
crisps – I don't – and I've tried every
lotion and cream around. Nothing seems
to help. I have to wear really thick
foundation to try to hide them. Will this
make things worse?

Leah, age 13

Spots are a fact of life for many teens . . . your hormones are working overtime, and the skin is producing more oil than usual, which can lead to spots. Great, huh? For Chloe, an over-the-counter lotion designed to control spotty skin should help – look for one containing benzoyl peroxide for best results. Greasy hair can be a problem for the same kind of reasons – keep the oil at bay by washing hair daily using a gentle formula shampoo that won't strip the hair.

Leah's skin problems are more serious. She's already tried over-the-counter treatments, with little success. Crisps and chocolate are not the healthiest foods on the planet, but there's no evidence that cutting them out will chase away teenage acne . . . the occasional treat definitely won't have any effect on your skin. As for hiding spots under a layer of foundation, if it helps Leah's confidence a little, then fine, but she should  choose an oil-free formula and cleanse her face religiously every night.

Never squeeze spots – even with clean fingers – as this can cause scarring. To beat teen acne, Leah must see her doctor. He/she can offer lotions, gels or tablets to help sort the problem, though there is no quick fix. Whatever the treatment, Leah will need to give it at least three months before she can expect to see an improvement.

It's important to keep going back to the doctor until the problem is sorted.

Can you help me, Cathy?
I have a really embarrassing problem
. . . I seem to be sweating a lot. I use a bodyspray, but it doesn't really help, and sometimes I actually get dark stains on my clothes. I'm worried that people will notice.

Amy, age 11

Cathy
Our friend has a problem with BO – she seems to wear the same school top for several days running, and she just smells really stale and sweaty. Some of the boys in class call her names behind her back, and even the teachers have

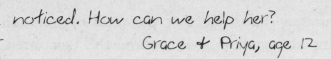

noticed. How can we help her?

Grace & Priya, age 12

Little kids don't sweat much, but once puberty sets in things change – big style. Underarm perspiration can be a problem, making you feel sticky and whiffy, and that's not good news.

Grace and Priya's friend – and Amy too – may be making some basic mistakes. Once you hit puberty, you need to shower every day, if possible, to stay fresh and confident, and if you can do this in the morning, better still. Dry off thoroughly and allow your body to cool down a little before applying antiperspirant deodorant to underarms. Note that a bodyspray is not the same thing – it'll give you a spritz of perfume, but no protection from perspiration. Whether you use a spray or a roll-on, it needs to say antiperspirant deodorant on the front!

It's also essential to wear clean underwear every day, and wear a fresh school shirt, if possible. Natural fibres like cotton and wool allow your body to breathe, so are better for staying confident. There may still be times when you perspire a little – when nervous, for example – but sticking to these rules will make sure you keep your cool.

Grace and Priya can help their friend by

bringing up the subject of personal hygiene and talking about their own routines. Their friend will, hopefully, get the message. Grace and Priya should also tell their guidance teacher about the teasing and ask him/her to keep an eye on things.

Mixed-Up Feelings

Hey Cathy
My best friend seems to be moody all the time these days. One minute she's laughing, the next she gets all snappy and stressy. It's driving me mad!
                    Tyler, age 10

Dear Cathy
I don't know what's up with me lately, but my moods are all over the place. Silly things can make me tearful and sensitive, and at other times I find myself getting stroppy and crabby for no reason at all. My family are getting fed up with me, but I don't know what to do!
                    Louise, age 12

When your hormones are going crazy, your moods can be crazy too. Many girls have mood swings at puberty, especially in the week just before their period.

Tyler needs to try to be patient with her friend – she's either struggling with mood swings, or she has a few problems at home. Tyler could try talking to her and seeing if there's anything she can do to help – but even just taking a step back from things and refusing to take the stressy moods personally can help.

Louise needs to see that she's not the only one going through all this . . . and accept that hormones are responsible. She's not going mad, just going through puberty! Being aware of what's happening can help – when Louise feels herself getting sad or stroppy, she can remind herself what's behind the mood and maybe pull back a little. Louise can also let her family know she's aware of the mood swings and doing her best to control them – this should help them to help her.

Dear Cathy
I hate being a teenager. I just don't feel
like me any more, and I hate my body – it

seems so big and clumsy and annoying. I wish I could be little again, and not have to worry about bras and boys and periods. Am I the only one who wants to turn the clock back?

Ruth, age 14

Cathy, please help me!
I can't seem to stop worrying lately. I worry that something bad might happen to my family, or that I might get ill and die, and sometimes when I watch the news I cry over things that are happening even though they're miles and miles away. I didn't realize the world was such a scary place. I never used to feel like this. What's going on?

Krissi, age 12

Growing up isn't just about the physical stuff. You're changing in all kinds of ways, and fast, and this can take some getting used to. It just takes a while

for your head to catch up with all the changes your body is making! We all have moments, like Ruth, when we'd like to give up and go back to when life was simpler, but that's just not possible! Accepting yourself as you are now is the only way forward.

Ruth is still the same person as she always was, just a little older. Her feelings of irritation, clumsiness and confusion are not unusual – many of her friends will have moments when they feel the same, and if Ruth tries talking to them about this, she may not feel so alone.

Krissi is experiencing another aspect of growing up – she's seeing the world around her, perhaps for the first time, and not liking what she sees. Growing up means realizing that your parents are only human and cannot protect you from everything in life, although they will try. Sometimes, bad things happen – scary things like illness and death and war and hunger.

Krissi worries that she cannot protect her family from these dangers, which obviously makes her feel very emotional and helpless. Realizing that the world is not a perfect place is bound to be frightening, but Krissi is not seeing the whole picture. Yes, there are bad things out there, but there are many, many good things as well. Love, kindness, community, friendship, family – these can keep us strong through good times and bad. And the world is a beautiful, amazing and awe-inspiring place too. Look for the good things, not the bad. There are plenty of them, I promise!

Feeling that you have the troubles of the world on your shoulders is a phase many teens go through, but it will pass. Life isn't big and bad and scary – it's a gift, and we owe it to ourselves not to waste a single minute.

OK, so period pains, spots, sweat problems and mood swings are not a whole bunch of fun, but although they can sometimes be a part of growing up, they are definitely temporary. They will ease off with time . . . honest!

Helpbox

Read It . . .

* *It's a Girl Thing* by Lisa Clark (Macmillan) – the coolest ever growing-up guide!
* *Wise Guides: Periods* by Charlotte Owen (Hodder)

* *Everything You Ever Wanted to Ask About . . . Periods* by Tricia Kreitman, Dr Fiona Finlay & Dr Rosemary Jones (Piccadilly)
* *What's Happening to My Body?* by Lynda Madaras (Newmarket Press)
* *My Body, Myself* by Lynda Madaras (Newmarket Press)
* *Girls Only* by Vic Parker (Hodder)

Websites:

www.stopspots.org.uk – for information, advice and support on coping with teenage acne
www.childrenfirst.nhs.uk – check out the kids or teens sites for lots of info on health and puberty-related issues.

Cathy's Books ... Published by Puffin

* *Shine On, Daizy Star* – boobs, bras and growing up . . .

3. Boys, Boys, Boys

Are boys an alien species? No, although sometimes they act that way! Growing-up is hard enough without the whole boy-thing to complicate matters . . . but then again, boys can be a nice complication. Hmmm. Hormones have a lot to answer for!

One day, the mop-headed boy who sits behind you in maths is a major pain who flicks paper pellets at you with his ruler and teases you about your freckles . . . the next, everything has changed. Your cheeks flush pink and you feel warm all over and slightly dizzy whenever he looks your way. Your heart races at the very sight of him. Are you ill? No, just crushing on him, big style!

Falling in love can be the best thing ever, but it opens up a whole new box of tricks when it comes to problems, worries and heartaches . . .

First Crush

Dear Cathy

I am in love with a boy in my class, but he doesn't seem to know I'm alive. He's so cute and all the girls fancy him, but how can I get him to notice ME?

Sarita, age 11

Hello Cathy

I am obsessed with Robert Pattinson from the film *Twilight*. My room is plastered with posters and I watch the DVD over and over. I love him, but how can I ever get to meet him?

Alyssa, age 13

Please help me, Cathy!

We have a new French teacher who is really young and cool. I dream about him all the time and imagine what it would be like to be going out with him. Please don't tell me this is a crush – I've never felt like this before!

Toni, age 12

What's the difference between a crush and real-life love? A crush can be intense, painful, all-consuming – but it's a one-way feeling. Often, the boy you're crushing on has no idea how you feel, or, if he does, just doesn't feel the same. A crush is a rehearsal for real-life love, a safe way to explore the feelings involved without acting on them. It's a practice run for the real thing.

Sarita is crushing on someone in her class, but she's in love with the idea of love rather than the boy himself. That's fine, as long as Sarita doesn't expect any more than that – the boy she likes may not feel the same way, and may not even be ready for a girlfriend.

Falling for someone can be a very random thing sometimes . . . the boy you like doesn't even know you exist, no matter how hard you try to catch his attention. And all of that time, it's possible a different boy is crushing on you – maybe a boy you couldn't fancy in a million years! There's just no logic in it . . . sadly!

Maybe the boy Sarita likes will fall for her too, but probably not . . . and there's nothing she can do to change that. Sarita should enjoy the crush while it lasts . . . no strings attached.

Alyssa knows her feelings for Robert Pattinson are a crush, but they are so intense it's hard for her to accept that. Falling for someone famous is a classic way to explore the highs and lows of attraction. Your crush can't let you down because he's safely out of reach . . . and he's always going to be perfect in your eyes because you can never really know the 'real' him. Besides, your imagination can fill in all the gaps until you're living in a real fantasy world.

Fantasy is fine, but if Alyssa starts trying to turn the dream into reality she is heading for heartache. When a crush begins to hurt you more than it makes you happy, it's time to let go, stop feeding the fantasy and step back into the real world again.

Fancying a teacher – or any older man – can be another part of growing up. Again, it's all about experiencing those feelings in a no-risk way because the person you're crushing on is way out of reach. Like it or not, what Toni describes is a classic crush . . . and that's the way it has to stay. Trying to turn a crush on an older man into reality is a fast track to disaster for everyone concerned. If Toni tried to tell this teacher how she felt, the end result would probably be major embarrassment – bad news.

Once a crush starts to control your life and make you unhappy, you need to get tough and let it go. Pretty soon, you'll fall for a boy who likes you too, and that's when things start to get really interesting . . . .

Taking Your Time 🌸🌸🌸🌸🌸🌸

Cathy
A boy at school has asked me out.
Everyone says he's lush, but I'm not
sure whether I want a boyfriend right
now . . .
                Jo, age 11

Hello Cathy
All of my friends have had boyfriends
except for me. I feel so left out, and
I worry that no boy will ever fancy me.
How can I get a boyfriend?
                        Kerri, age 13

Dating is not a game – or a race. Don't accept a date unless you really like the boy and feel you are ready for a relationship, or it'll end in tears. Jo is flattered that a cute boy likes her enough to ask her out, but she also knows she doesn't feel the same way about him and isn't ready for a boyfriend yet. If she's smart, Jo will tell the boy that she likes him a lot as a mate, but isn't ready to take things further. That lets her off the hook without hurting his feelings.

Jo is right not to be pressured into dating just for the sake of it. Don't feel you have to have a boyfriend just because your friends do . . . that's NOT a good enough reason! It's way better to wait until you meet someone you really like, who feels the same way. Kind of obvious, really!

Kerri is feeling bad because it seems that everyone else but her has a boyfriend. She's so keen to start dating she doesn't much care *who* she goes out with, and boys can sense that – it's not exactly flattering! Desperation is never attractive. Kerri needs to slow down. Having a boyfriend is not like having the latest CD or pair of jeans . . . a boy is a real person, with feelings, not an accessory designed to make you look and feel better.

When the right boy comes along, Kerri will know it – and it will be worth the wait.

Dear Cathy
I am crazy about a boy called Kyle. I'd like to ask him out, but I'm scared he'll say no . . .
Kayleigh, age 13

Cathy

There's a boy I like a LOT. We used to be friends back in primary school, but these days I just get really shy and tongue-tied when he's around. My friends have offered to tell him how I feel . . . is that a good idea?

Lorna, age 13

Asking someone out is scary – whether you're a boy or a girl! Kayleigh needs to get to know Kyle as a friend before she takes things any further . . . the two can get to know each other a little, suss out whether they have anything in common and whether there's a spark of attraction there. If so, the chances are both will start sending out subtle signals that they like each other – what we usually call flirting, I guess!

It's much easier to ask someone out if you think there's a chance they might say yes. Kayleigh should keep things light and friendly, perhaps asking Kyle if he's seen the latest film or if he's ever been skating, and asking casually if he'd like to go along some time. If he does turn her down, she can shrug off the rejection and do her best to take it in her stride. There are all kinds of reasons why someone might choose not to accept a date

– it doesn't have to be a personal thing!

Falling for someone can make you feel awkward and shy when they're around, but Lorna should try to beat the blushes and get chatting to the boy she likes. This is usually a better bet than letting friends take charge of things . . . often a fast-track to disaster! Why? News of your crush will spread like wildfire, which can be embarrassing. And facing up to a posse of loud and possibly pushy friends could send your crush running in the opposite direction! Not good.

Think about it – if you can't find the courage to say hello to the boy you like, would you have the courage to go on a date with him?

Hey Cathy
My boyfriend and I talk a lot on Bebo and MSN, but at school we're really shy with each other. And we never actually go on a date. Is this normal?

Nadine, age 12

Cathy
My boyfriend always takes me to the park or to the chip shop and it

gets a bit boring sometimes. What else could we do? Neither of us have much money!

Marley, age 14

When you're young, like Nadine, going out with someone may not mean romantic dates and red roses. Often, it's just a way of saying you like someone – the actual 'going out' bit might not add up to much at all! If Nadine and her boyfriend are happy chatting on Bebo and MSN, that's OK – they're still getting to know each other, slowly. If it works for you, then it's fine!

Marley and her boyfriend are going on dates, but they're in a bit of a rut . . . some imagination could liven things up for them. Marley could plan a picnic, a bike ride, a day at the ice rink or swimming pool, even a film night at her place with DVDs and popcorn! The two could have a 'posh' dinner at the local greasy spoon diner, hire a rowing boat on the river, feed the ducks, go to the zoo, go to a museum or art gallery . . . even fly a kite! Doing cool/crazy things together gives you lots of great memories to look back on . . . and it's fun!

They could even take inspiration from some of my books . . .

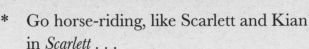

* Go horse-riding, like Scarlett and Kian in *Scarlett* . . .

* Look at the stars or watch a firework display like Cat & Mouse in *Lucky Star*...

* Picnic in the park like Anya and Dan in *Angel Cake* (but not after midnight, OK?!!!)

* Take a bike ride to the beach and send a message in a bottle like Paul and Hannah in *Driftwood* . . .

* Go to a mini music festival like Dizzy and Finn in *Dizzy* . . . or set up your own mini gig!

Love Hurts

Help!

One of the coolest boys in my year has asked me out. I said yes, but I'm really nervous because I've never had a boyfriend or kissed anyone before. What if I make a mess of it? What if our

teeth crash together or I can't work out
how to breathe or something? Help!

Tilda, age 13

Dear Cathy
A boy from the year above me
chatted me up at a party last week.
We ended up kissing and he wanted
to go a bit further, but I said no.
Now he's telling everyone I'm a baby
who can't even kiss . . . I'm so
upset!
   Gina, age 14

Tilda's worry is one many girls share. That first kiss
can seem scary, but the key is to relax and enjoy it.
Everyone has to go through that first kiss sometime
. . . it's nothing to feel shy about! If a kiss is coming
at you, part your lips slightly, tilt your head and
close your eyes . . . then do what comes naturally!
Slow, gentle movements are best, and the more you
practise the better you'll be. Tilda's boyfriend won't
mind if she's not an expert – in fact, he'll be happy
to help with the practice!

Gina has had a very bad experience. The boy she kissed was a loser, and when he didn't get his own way he lashed out at her by spreading nasty gossip. Luckily, most people who hear the gossip will realize things weren't quite the way they sound. Gossip like this has a way of backfiring on those who spread it.

Gina knows she did the right thing here . . . you should never, ever let anyone push you into doing anything you are not happy with or ready for. Gina should hold her head high and blank the nasty comments. Like most gossip, it will soon be forgotten.

Dear Cathy
I met this guy and really fancied him. Then my friend Nessa met him and now they are going out, but I still have feelings for him! Nessa isn't even pretty! Should I flirt with him and tell him how I feel? I hate being in Year Eight!
          Sophie, age 12

Hiya Cathy
I have fallen for my best friend's boyfriend, and I think he feels

the same. He sent me some texts saying he really likes me. I feel really torn . . . what should I do?

Kelsie, age 14

Sophie and Kelsie both have the same lesson to learn here – friendship comes before boys, every time. The minute you let a boy come between you, you're in trouble . . . boys will come and go, but friendships can be forever.

Sophie met a boy and fancied him, but the spark wasn't there for him, or he'd be dating Sophie, not her friend. Sophie clearly feels this is unfair, but the truth is, love isn't fair . . . there is often no logic behind who fancies who! If Sophie starts flirting and trying to stir things up, she's more likely to wreck her friendship with Nessa than anything else . . . and for what? A boy who doesn't fancy her anyway.

Kelsie needs to accept that her mate's boyfriend is strictly off-limits. OK, it's flattering to know someone fancies you, but this boy is bad news . . . sending flirty texts to other girls when you're in a relationship? Trust me, if he can do it to Kelsie's mate, he'd do it to Kelsie too.

Dear Cathy
I think I have fallen in love, and it's not good because I have fallen in love with another girl. I am terrified someone will find out. I feel such a freak.

Eve, age 13

Many teens go through a stage of feeling attracted to the same sex. This doesn't mean you're gay, just curious, and exploring the whole love/lust/ attraction thing. However, for some this isn't just a stage – it's a part of who you are.

Eve is confused and upset by her feelings, but she shouldn't feel ashamed of them or label herself a freak. Falling for someone of the same sex is nothing to feel bad about. Whether Eve chooses to tell anyone how she is feeling is a tough decision – if the girl she likes doesn't feel the same way, she may well feel threatened or scared. Eve's best plan is to tread carefully until she's sure of herself and her sexuality. She can talk to her guidance tutor or school counsellor for more support and help.

Breaking Up ✿✿✿✿✿✿✿

Dear Cathy
I've been going out with a boy for three weeks. I like him, but as a friend, nothing more. I hate it when he gets all smoochy and romantic. I want to finish with him, but I don't want to hurt his feelings.

Alice, age 12

Dear Cathy
What are your tips on getting over someone? My boyfriend just dumped me and it feels like the end of the world to me. I don't even understand what I did wrong!

Erin, age 14

When you're a teenager, you're changing, growing and learning all the time . . . and that means love just doesn't last forever. Handling break-ups is a part of the learning process.

Alice knows she has to end this relationship – the longer she lets things drag on, the harder it will be. A quick, clean break will mean less hurt in the long run. Alice should find a quiet place to talk to her boyfriend, and explain, kindly but firmly, that although she likes him as a friend, things aren't going to go any further than that.

If you ever need to finish a relationship, always do it in person. Never let a friend do it for you, or be tempted to do it by text, phone or email. You owe it to your soon-to-be ex to be honest and direct – treat him the way you'd like to be treated if things were the other way around.

It may be hard to end a relationship, but being dumped is harder still. Like Erin, you may still care about your ex and find it hard to understand why things have ended. Erin feels she must be in some way to blame, but the chances are that the relationship has simply run its course. Her ex has moved on – and now she must too.

So how do you get over a break-up? Remember the good times, but don't forget the bad times too . . . if things had been perfect, it wouldn't have ended like this. Feel sad – feel angry if you need to – and then move on. It's an ending, sure, but also the beginning of something new perhaps! Stay busy with friends, family, school and fun . . . don't feel sorry for yourself. No relationship is a waste of time – you learn from every one of them, even if you get your fingers burnt.

Helpbox

Cathy's Books . . . Published by Puffin

*   *GingerSnaps* – when your best friend doesn't
    approve of the boy you like . . .
*   *Angel Cake* – falling for a bad boy . . . and
    finding that your love rival is the school
    mean-girl . . .
*   *Scarlett* – cool, mysterious, kind . . . is Kian
    too good to be true?
*   *Dizzy* – can a boy mate become a boyfriend?
*   *Sundae Girl* – Carter is annoying, clumsy,
    loyal, persistent – and seriously romantic . . .
*   *Lucky Star* – a boy from a rough high-rise
    estate and a girl from the posh side of town –
    what happens when opposites attract!
*   *Driftwood* – when the boy you like doesn't
    seem to feel the same . . .

4. School Daze

Schooldays are the best days of your life? Er, right . . . whoever thought up that little phrase clearly hadn't been inside a classroom for some time! School can be cool, but more often it's just plain hard work – and not just in class, either.

Unless you happen to be home-educated, the chances are you spend most of your time at school . . . and if you're not happy there, that has to be a problem. So how can you sort your school hassles and learn to take it all in your stride?

School's Cool!

Hi Cathy
I am starting high school after the summer and I can't help thinking the worst even though I try not to. I loved primary school, but I'm worried that I'll be really out of my depth at secondary.
                              Jacqui, age 11

Dear Cathy
Do you have any advice on going to a

comprehensive school? I'm going into Year Seven and I am really scared. My friends will be going to the same one, but we won't know which forms we're in until the first day back. What if they split us up? The more I think about my new school, the more upset I get.

— Ellis, age 11

Changing schools is a big milestone. It can feel like the end of childhood, and saying goodbye to primary school is often an emotional time. Jacqui needs to change her attitude to secondary school and start seeing the pros rather than the cons!

Starting high school is a new beginning . . . and that has to be a good thing! A fresh start is something to look forward to . . . . new friends, new teachers, new subjects and LOTS of new opportunities. OK, the school campus will almost certainly be bigger, and you may get lost a few times in the first week – but every Year Seven (or S1 if you are in Scotland) will have the same problem! The first few days are bound to be confusing, but trust me, pretty soon you'll know where you are going.

Another big change is adjusting to being

the youngest and smallest in the school again, after a year of being a cool, confident Year Six (or P7) at primary. It's kind of daunting to be the new kid in a crispy-new uniform and shiny shoes, surrounded by gruff, towering lads and curvy, grown-up girls in lip gloss and eyeliner! Don't be scared of the older kids, though – they look pretty sussed, but they're still kids underneath! Most will take time out to help you if you get lost or have a problem. Sometimes, the scariest-looking kids can be the kindest!

Everyone feels a little out of their depth at secondary school, but this feeling rarely lasts for more than a few days. Jacqui can make things easier for herself by listing the things she's looking forward to about switching schools . . . making new mates, discovering new subjects, inspiring new teachers, cool after-school and lunchtime clubs and being treated as more grown-up and independent are all definite plus points! If she catches herself thinking negative thoughts, she can banish them by repeating the list of things to look forward to. By the time term starts, she'll be raring to go!

Ellis too is letting fears cloud her mind and spoil her summer. There are no guarantees you'll be put in a form with your friends, but most secondary schools will do their best to keep you together. If you are split up, try to see it as a bonus . . . You'll soon make new mates in your form group, yet be able to meet up with your old friends at break and lunchtime.

When I started high school, my three best friends from primary all went to different schools. Unlucky! I was quite anxious that first day, and ended up sitting in a seat by myself, feeling very self-conscious. A few minutes into form time, there was a knock on the door and a new girl appeared . . . her name hadn't been on the form lists, but she was part of our class. She looked around, scoping out the empty desks, and opted to sit by me.

Jennie came from a different school and didn't know anyone at all, either, but she quickly became my new best friend. Pretty soon we found ourselves part of a close-knit group of six, none of whom had known each other in primary. We were all very different, and maybe wouldn't have looked like ideal 'friendship' material, but we bonded and stayed close all the way through high school.

If Jacqui and Ellis stop dwelling on fears and negative thoughts, they will start to see secondary school as the cool new start it really is . . . sorted!

Teacher's Pet?

Dear Cathy
I really like my new teacher. We get on
really well and I'm learning loads this year,
but some of the kids have started calling me
a swot and a teacher's pet! I hate this, but
I don't know what to do about it!

Shiva, age 10

Cathy
I love your books - reading is
probably my favourite thing, and
I always have my nose in a book.
Some kids tease me and say I'm a
geek and a loser. Why can't they
leave me alone?

Joss, age 12

Shiva's classmates are probably envious of her
enthusiasm and success this year . . . by calling
her a swot and a teacher's pet, they are trying to
make her feel bad for working hard. Shiva needs to
shrug off the negative comments – she should feel
proud of her achievements! If the teasing is getting

to her, Shiva can have a quiet word with her teacher and explain what's happening. By sharing the praise and attention with Shiva's classmates, her teacher can make sure everyone stays keen and motivated.

Joss doesn't need me to tell her that reading is cool . . . she knows! It's a great feeling to open the pages of a book and escape into a whole new world . . . and of course, kids who read a lot get better marks at school because they are learning all the time without even realizing it!

When I was twelve, like Joss, I was a bookworm, but rarely took my books into school, in case I got teased. All that changed when I was given the book *Watership Down* by Richard Adams. If you've never read it, *Watership Down* is the story of a bunch of rabbits who have all kinds of adventures. Back then, the book had a big picture of a rabbit on the cover, and I wasn't sure if this was the kind of book I wanted to be seen with at the age of twelve. I started reading and was hooked right away . . . I couldn't put the book down all weekend.

On Monday morning, I couldn't resist taking it to school, in case I got the chance to read it in between lessons. Our English teacher was late that afternoon, and while everyone chatted noisily outside the classroom, I edged away, sat on a quiet window sill and opened my book. I was careful to hold a hand over the cover, in case anyone saw me reading it!

I was miles away, wrapped up in the story, when the worst thing ever happened. The cutest boy in our year walked up and asked me what I was reading. I went the colour of a beetroot, but I had no option but to show him the book – and to my amazement, he grinned and said, '*Watership Down*? That's the best book I've ever read!'

I learnt a really important lesson that day – never, ever be ashamed of reading. Seriously. (And if you've never read *Watership Down*, give it a go – whatever your age!)

Joss is not a geek or a loser. She should blank the nasty comments, or, if that doesn't work, talk to her guidance tutor and get some adult support. It's cool to like learning . . . that's one lesson we could all do with swotting up on.

Teacher Trouble

Hello Cathy
Our English teacher has one or two kids in class he really likes, and they

get all the attention. He often says the rest of us are a washout, which upsets me because I used to love English. How can I make him see I'm trying as hard as I can?

Jill, age 13

Cathy
Have you ever had a teacher you didn't like? I have, and it's making my life a misery!

Charleen, age 14

One thing you should know about teachers – they're not perfect. Like the rest of us, teachers are only human – they make mistakes, mess up sometimes, and some of them are not as nice as others!

Jill's teacher may not mean to, but by dismissing most of his class as 'a washout' he is alienating them. Why should they try to impress a teacher who has already labelled them as losers? Jill is missing out on her favourite subject, which isn't fair. She and a friend could try talking to this teacher quietly after class one day, explaining that they are trying hard, but would love a little more support. Hopefully, he'll get the message!

Having a teacher you really don't like is very tough, as Charleen has discovered. I too had a teacher who made my life miserable, back in primary school. It's even worse if this happens to you at primary school because you only have the one teacher for every subject – there's no escape!!! My mum came in to talk to the teacher who was making me so unhappy, but even that didn't help . . . things didn't improve until she left to have a baby. Phew! Looking back, I wonder if she'd been having an especially stressful pregnancy, but still, I wish she hadn't chosen to take it out on us!

Charleen could try talking to her guidance tutor or year head, or getting her mum or dad to have a word with her teacher next Parents' Night. Those things may help, but often, all you can do is accept that you just won't hit it off with every teacher you come across. Luckily, you won't be stuck with them forever!

Dear Cathy
I really identify with your book
Driftwood. I like to dress a little bit
differently, but the teachers at my
school assume you're going to grow up to

be an axe-murderer if you dare to have a long fringe or a liking for black clothes. It's so unfair! There are kids here who smoke in the school loos and do all kinds of dodgy stuff, and the teachers don't even notice!

Binni, age 13

Hey
Why do teachers go crazy if you wear the tiniest bit of eyeshadow or vamp up the school uniform with a pair of lacy tights or a hipster belt? What's wrong with wanting to be cool?

Bexx, age 12

Binni has a point. Some teachers panic at the first sign of black eyeliner and dipping fringes, assuming that a taste for doom, gloom and antisocial behaviour will follow. Er, no!!! Young people just love to express themselves through clothes, and a pair of fingerless gloves are very unlikely to lead to a life of crime!

I agree with Binni – a little more time spent on sorting the real problems that exist in every school and a little less on hassling kids for wearing Converse or dyeing their hair might not be a bad thing. But that's just my opinion . . . and when I was a teacher, I sometimes got into trouble myself for *not* enforcing the uniform rules! Oops!

Why do teachers make such a big deal of school uniform? Well, all schools are different, but many believe that a strict school uniform code makes all pupils equal and creates a strong, smart identity for the school.

If Binni and Bexx don't agree with the uniform rules at their schools, they could try to start a discussion with the senior teachers and see whether things can be changed. Perhaps the school is looking for a uniform update? Get talking, get involved . . . you never know what you can achieve until you try!

Work It Out

Hey Cathy
At school I'm finding it really hard to keep up with the work. I struggle with things my friends find easy, and I can't cope with all

the homework because most of the time I
didn't understand the classwork! I can't tell
anyone about this — I'm too embarrassed.

Wendy, age 12

Hi Cathy
I hate maths. I just can't do it
at all, no matter how hard I try.
Now my mum has suggested getting
a private tutor and I can't bear
the thought of that. I wish I didn't
have to do it!

Jessica, age 13

If you're not coping with the workload, ask for help.
Wendy is scared to admit she has a problem, but
the longer she ignores it the worse it will get. The
teachers are there to help you, but they can't do
that unless you tell them you're struggling! Often,
teachers can work out why things are difficult and
offer support, extra classes, or even suggest a change
of group where the work is more on your level.

Asking for help doesn't mean you're stupid – just
the opposite. You're smart enough to know there's
a problem and to get some expert help on side to
sort it!

Jessica's problem is one I really identify with. I too hated maths, especially in secondary school. I struggled with every maths homework, bombed in every test and cried at home over some especially challenging topics. My teachers often wrote 'See me' in red pen at the bottom of my workbooks, but I never did because I was scared that meant I was in trouble. I realize now they were only trying to help me!

I was very lucky – with support at home and a very patient teacher, I scraped a pass in my final maths exam. I'm glad I did, because like it or not, maths is one of the most important subjects to have under your belt . . . it can open a lot of doors.

I'm still not confident with numbers. I recently met a maths teacher at a party who told me that with the right attitude and the right teacher, everyone can learn maths. I think he's probably right. Jessica should jump at the chance to get some private maths tuition – a different approach to the subject could make it a whole lot less scary. She should also tell her teachers at school she needs more support.

My last piece of advice for Jessica? Try to turn your attitude around and believe that you can do maths . . . labelling yourself as rubbish at something is one sure-fire way to make sure you will be. I wish

I'd known that when I was twelve . . . it could have saved me a lot of heartache.

Cathy
I've just started high school and I get quite a bit of homework, but there's nowhere quiet for me to do it. The TV is always on downstairs and I share a room with my sister, and she never gives me any peace. Nightmare!

Naseem, age 11

Dear Cathy
I am not very organized with my homework. I always think I have loads of time to get it done, but then I forget and end up trying to do it at the bus stop before school. I'm always in trouble because of this.

Lyddi, age 11

Homework . . . you work hard at school, and then they expect you to do more at home too? Well, yes, 'fraid so. Homework is the best way ever of making sure you've understood something properly, of practising a difficult skill or task and fixing the facts firmly in your mind. It also teaches you how to work under your own steam, and this gets more and more important as you get older.

One thing you do need is a quiet place to work. Naseem needs to talk to her family and look for a compromise here. Can the TV be switched off for an hour or so each evening, or can Naseem have some quiet time in her room to work? It means changing things around a little, but it's important for Naseem's school career, so it's worth looking for a solution.

Lyddi's problem is lack of organization. Now she's at secondary school, she needs to take responsibility for homework and set aside time to do it every day – she should keep a homework diary or notebook to jot down what has to be done and when it needs to be in by. I always liked to get my homework out of the way as soon as I could – straight after school, while it was still fresh in my mind. Sometimes, I'd do a rough draft of an essay and then copy it out and tidy it up the next night – I still do several drafts of a story now! Checking over homework or doing a second draft makes sure you always hand in your best work – and get the best grade for it!

If you leave homework to the last moment, you'll end up rushing it and handing in something that's not your best work. And sometimes, as Lyddi has discovered, you'll forget it completely and pay the price . . .

Hi Cathy

I am very worried about my end-of-term tests. I know my parents expect me to do well, and I'm scared I will let them down. I lie awake at night thinking about it all. What can I do?

Mariam, age 10

Cathy

I've been a fan of your books for ages. I don't know why, but I feel I can talk to you because you understand teenagers and what we go through. I am so worried about my standard grade exams. There is so much to revise I don't know where to start . . . I feel like giving up right now.

Iona, age 14

Exams and tests are major stress points for the young people who write and email me. I used to worry about exams too, but the testing starts at a much younger age these days, so the pressure starts earlier too.

Mariam is worried about letting her parents down, and that fear is eating away at her confidence. I guarantee that her parents just want her to do the best she can. Mariam needs to talk to her parents and explain how anxious she's feeling . . . her family can help her to get things in perspective.

Iona is so overwhelmed at all the revision she has to do that she can't see a way forward – it seems easier to give in to panic than to actually make a start on the work. Revision is no picnic, but it is the key to exam success . . . get organized early on and you'll be prepared when test time comes around. So how do you do it?

Check with each teacher just what you need to revise, and ask for any help they can offer. Practise answering exam-type questions, for instance, so you know how to approach the exam paper itself.

Make a revision timetable, slotting in time to revise each subject, and start revising a couple of months before the exams. It sounds a lot, but giving yourself plenty of time means you can take it slowly and revise thoroughly. If you try to cram your

revision in the night before the exam, you've only yourself to blame when it all goes pear-shaped!

Allow slots of one to two hours for each subject, and tackle one or two subjects each night. Take a break now and then for a snack, a rest and some exercise . . . even walking the dog round the block can help chase away the cobwebs, and you'll come back to your revision feeling much more alert.

Don't just flick through your books and expect the information to sink in . . . make notes and lists, copy out key facts, highlight important points. When I was revising back in high school, I'd copy my notes out several times to fix the facts in my head, and sometimes record facts on to a tape to play back. You can also get study-guides for your subjects, check out revision aids on the Internet, study with a friend and quiz each other, work through past papers, attend after-school study groups . . . whatever works for you.

Don't leave it to chance, and don't aim to just scrape through – this is your future we're talking about. Some people enjoy the buzz of an exam, and do their best in a high-pressure situation. Others go to pieces, panic and forget what they've learnt . . . not so good. If you get nervous, try some slow, deep breathing to stop the panic in its tracks and tell yourself you are prepared . . . you CAN do it.

However nervous you are, get a good night's sleep and eat a healthy breakfast before every exam . . . your brain can't perform if your body is running on empty.

Once you're in the actual test or exam, read the questions through carefully, take a deep breath and do your best . . . that's all anyone can ask of you.

School Blues ✽ ✽ ✽ ✽ ✽ ✽ ✽

Cathy please help . . .
My mum has been ill and things
are difficult at home. My school
work is slipping because of this,
and I'm afraid it will mess up my
future. Plus, I'm often tired in
class and my teachers are getting
really hacked off with me.

Gita, age 13

Dear Cathy
My mum and dad are fighting all the time these days. I don't seem to be able to concentrate at school. Sometimes, I lose

my temper with friends because their worries just seem so trivial compared to this. I just don't see the point of school any more.

Lorri, age 12

Gita and Lorri both need to talk to their guidance tutors, class teachers or school counsellors, and soon. When things go wrong at home, school work often skids out of control, and that means trouble. Once you let things slide, it's very hard to catch up – better to ask for help now.

At times like these, the school needs to know there is a problem – not just so they can help with work, but so they can make sure you're OK in other ways too. If the teachers know why Gita is often tired in class, for example, they won't hassle her about it; and if they know why Lorri is snappy and fed up, they can help her too.

It might help Gita and Lorri to talk to a trusted teacher or counsellor about what's going on at home too. School shouldn't be an added worry when things go wrong at home – it can be a support.

Dear Cathy
I have just read your book Lucky

Star. I am just like Mouse - I have dyslexia. I am a very slow reader, but I love reading because when I read I don't worry about school or anything, I can go where the book takes me and be anything or anyone I want to be. Thanks for making Mouse someone I can relate to. It's nice to know people like you know about dyslexia and how it stinks to be in Special Ed.

Tamara, age 13

*

Tamara is right, it's tough to be dyslexic. One of the toughest things is that others don't always understand, and assume that because you have problems with reading and writing, you can't be smart. Wrong – I have several friends who are dyslexic, and they're among the smartest people I know! It takes real determination to succeed when you're dyslexic because you see and recognize letters and words in a jumbled, confusing way. This makes reading and writing a huge challenge.

Never judge others because they need support in class or go to Special Ed classes – if anything, you should respect them for what they have achieved in spite of their difficulties. I loved writing about Mouse in *Lucky Star* – a bright, creative character who just happened to have problems with reading and writing! I also loved Tamara's letter, as it showed that it's worth persevering even if reading is hard for you – the buzz of escaping into a book is a great reward!

So, school's not perfect, I guess, but if you work with the system it's a whole lot easier. There might still be things you want to change, but you have more chance of doing that from the inside . . . wish there was a school mag or a drama group or a green club? Get together with some friends, talk to the teachers and set one up! Hate school lunches? Think of ways they could be improved, get some support from your classmates and talk to the Head – and the kitchen staff! Dream of having a school prom? Get organizing!

If you're not coping as well as you'd like, find a couple of teachers you can talk to and get some support . . . school is all about teamwork, about working together to get results.

Helpbox

Read It . . .

* *In School Stay Cool* – booklet on starting secondary school . . . covering all the essentials (download a digital version for free, or go to the YoungMinds website for more info: *www.youngminds.org.uk*)
* *Get Better Grades* by Agnew/Barlow/Pascal/Skidmore (Piccadilly)
* *Going Up* by Jenny Alexander (A & C Black) – starting secondary school
* *Wise Guides: Exam Skills* by Kate Brooks (Hodder)
* *Mind Maps for Kids* by Tony Buzan (Harper Thorsons) – study skills

Websites:

www.buzzin.net/revision_tips – how to make learning fun . . . and effective!

www.childline.org.uk – sections on school, homework and exams

www.bbc.co.uk/schools/bitesize/ – help on revision for whichever level you are at

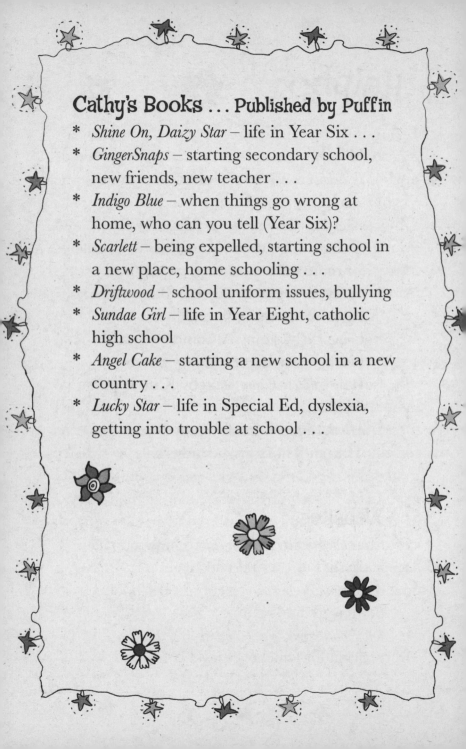

Cathy's Books ... Published by Puffin

* *Shine On, Daizy Star* – life in Year Six . . .
* *GingerSnaps* – starting secondary school, new friends, new teacher . . .
* *Indigo Blue* – when things go wrong at home, who can you tell (Year Six)?
* *Scarlett* – being expelled, starting school in a new place, home schooling . . .
* *Driftwood* – school uniform issues, bullying
* *Sundae Girl* – life in Year Eight, catholic high school
* *Angel Cake* – starting a new school in a new country . . .
* *Lucky Star* – life in Special Ed, dyslexia, getting into trouble at school . . .

5. Beat Bullying

I get more letters and emails about bullying than any other subject, and I've written about it in several of my books because I know it is a big worry for some of you.

Bullying is nothing new. Your parents and grandparents will remember bullying incidents from their early years, but they may say things like 'It didn't do me any harm,' or 'It's a part of growing up.' Bullying is a part of growing up for some people, but it shouldn't be – ever. And it can cause a lot of harm.

It is not OK to push people around, treat them like dirt, call them cruel names or hurt them. If we accept this kind of behaviour as normal, the bullies will grow up thinking it's OK to treat others like this. Whether you're being bullied, have been bullied in the past, seen a friend suffer or have even bullied people yourself, it's time to call a halt. We can stop bullying, but we have to accept that it's wrong and act together to make it unacceptable.

Don't Pick On Me

Dear Cathy

I've just read *GingerSnaps* and the way Ginger was treated back when she was in primary school was exactly like what happened to me. Things are better now, but I wanted to ask, were you ever bullied at school? You write about it as if you really understand.

Mischa, age 14

I wasn't bullied at school, but I was teased . . . luckily, it never went any further. At primary, I was pretty confident and knew how to stick up for myself, but by the time I was eleven, things changed. Suddenly, I stood out from the crowd – I was growing up, literally! At eleven years old I was five feet eight inches tall and towered above my classmates. I towered above most of my teachers too!

I was called names and jokers liked to ask what the weather was like 'up there'. I hated the teasing and the attention. I hunched my shoulders and wished I could be invisible. My confidence had been dented, big style, and that shyness stayed with me for years. I thought I might go on growing forever, but five feet eight was as tall as

I ever got . . . and I love being that height now. I just wish I'd got here a little more gradually!

Anyone who stands out from the crowd and lacks confidence can be a target for bullies, but I was lucky – because I towered over the bullies as well, they never pushed me too far. That's one of the interesting points about bullies . . . they tend to pick on those smaller and weaker than themselves.

It could have been me, though, and maybe that's why I have an empathy with anyone who has been picked on. As an adult, I taught art in both secondary and primary schools, and saw many examples of bullying along the way. In my twelve years as agony aunt for *Shout* mag, I heard yet more stories of how bullying could wreck lives and destroy confidence, and even now the letters and emails continue to pour in from readers who are trying hard to break free from the bullies.

Cathy
The boys in my class are always calling me names like Speccy and Four Eyes, just because I wear glasses. It really annoys me, but my mum tells me to just ignore it. How can I?
                    Millie, age 10

Hi Cathy

I've got my own style of dressing and some of the girls in my year call me 'emo' or 'goth-girl', which really bugs me. How can I get them to leave me alone?

Lois, age 14

Millie and Lois are being teased rather than bullied, but they're not handling the teasing too well. If you allow yourself to get wound up by comments like this, they can easily cross the line from teasing into bullying. How do you stop that from happening? As Millie's mum suggests, you stop reacting.

It sounds simple, but blanking this kind of name-calling really can work. People like to get a reaction when they tease – a blush, a frown, an angry reply. If you don't react at all, or just smile quietly as if the name doesn't bother you, the jokers are likely to give up after a while and find new victims who are easier to wind up. Give it a go – imagine an invisible wall around you, protecting you from the nasty names. Act like you don't care and gradually you may find you actually do care less.

If ignoring the comments is not an option, try

laughing along with the jokers to take the sting out of their words. Those who tease others are often used to being teased themselves at home, and may not even realize they're hurting you. Show them that they don't bother you, or laugh off the comment – it's no big deal unless you allow it to be.

Please help, Cathy!
One of the girls in my class keeps calling me fat and ugly and says I might smash the mirror when I go to the loos. I don't understand what I've done wrong – why is she picking on me?
                    Rosa, age 11

Cathy.
I am like ginger in your book gingerSnaps . . . I get bullied because I have red hair. The thing that really gets to me is that a couple of other kids in the class

have red hair too, and nobody says anything to them. How come?

Janine, age 10

Why are some people targeted and not others? Bullies look for someone they can push around, someone they can get a reaction from. It's easy to pick on those who stand out from the crowd, those who are different in some way. If you have red hair, glasses, are overweight or small and skinny, have sticky-out ears, are extra clever, struggle with school work, belong to a different race/ culture/religion to the rest of the group . . . well, you could be singled out. But many people fit those categories and never get picked on at all! Why is that?

The bottom line is, bullies pick on people they get a reaction from, people who seem nervous, shy, weak or unsure of themselves. If you walk along with your shoulders slumped and your eyes on the ground, you're sending out a powerful message that you're anxious, awkward, scared. If you walk tall, smile and aren't afraid to look others in the eye, you send out a message that you're confident and relaxed. Which type of person is most likely to attract the attention of a bully?

Make sure your body language is relaxed and walk tall – it helps. You may not feel confident, but if you act that way it's almost as good. Fake it till you make it! There are lots of tips for boosting your confidence in the next chapter too.

Sadly, it's often quiet, kind, sensitive types like Rosa and Janine who end up being bullied, perhaps because they're too nice to fight back. They may show their distress easily or even cry, which is the kind of reaction a bully loves. Rosa and Janine need to learn to stand up for themselves, but one thing is for sure – they've done nothing wrong, nothing to deserve the bullying.

The bully is the problem – not the victim.

Sticks and Stones

Hi Cathy
Some girls in my class seem to hate me. They treat me as though I'm disgusting and dirty, call me terrible names and try to turn the whole class against me. I'm so unhappy I could die.

Nikki, age 12

Hey Cathy
A gang of kids from the estate where
I live are picking on me and my friend.
They chase us and try to get money
off us, and last week they ripped my
blazer and kicked us and pulled our hair.
We're terrified.
                    Bel, age 11

Which kind of bullying is more serious: the kind
of verbal/emotional bullying that's happening to
Nikki, or the physical bullying that Bel and her
friend are struggling with?

Often, physical bullying is taken much more
seriously than emotional bullying. Bel and her
friend have proof of what's going on – cuts, bruises
and torn clothing – to show just how serious things
are. Bel and her friend are right to be scared.
They need to speak out, tell their parents and
contact the police – this kind of bullying cannot
be ignored.

How about Nikki? She isn't actually being hurt . . .
or is she? Maybe it's just that we can't see the scars
from this kind of bullying because they're buried

deep inside. Verbal and emotional bullying is every bit as serious as physical bullying, and needs to be tackled with just the same kind of urgency. The damage from this kind of treatment is very real. It destroys self-esteem, isolates and sometimes drives victims to suicide.

Parents and teachers sometimes repeat that old saying, 'Sticks and stones may break my bones, but words will never hurt me . . .' Well, emotional bullying may not break bones, but it breaks people inside, and that is just as dangerous. It needs to be taken just as seriously as physical bullying.

Dear Cathy
My friend is being picked on. I want to help her, but I'm scared the bully will target me too. What can I do?

Yasmine, age 12

Cathy
Some kids have been picking on me for months and the other day they just pushed me too far and I snapped. I shoved the bully and yelled and swore at her, and guess

what? I ended up being excluded.
It feels like nobody will listen and
everyone is against me, even the
teachers.

Shanice, age 13

Yasmine is scared to stick up for her friend in case it means she ends up being bullied too . . . but there's lots she can do to help. Just hanging out with her friend – with a few more friends in tow as well, if possible – may be enough to keep the bullies at bay. If you stick together, it's also easier to challenge the bullies and ask them why they're doing this . . .

Yasmine can help her friend to say 'no' to the bullies, to walk tall, hide her fear and act confident. She can also help her friend to speak out, going along with her to tell a teacher what's been going on.

Shanice tried fighting back – literally – and found herself in trouble. This doesn't seem fair – Shanice had been pushed to breaking point, but the teachers weren't looking too closely for the reasons behind her outburst. Fighting back is not a good idea. You may end up in trouble, like Shanice, or worse, you could end up getting very badly hurt. Violence is not the answer.

Shanice needs to turn this situation around by telling her teachers exactly why this scrap happened. She should write down a record of the bullying, tell her parents and go along with them to see her teachers. Hopefully, this situation can be sorted out.

Speaking Out

Dear Cathy

I'm being bullied and it has been going on for months. My friends say I should tell my parents and speak to a guidance teacher at school, but I just can't - if the bullies find out they'll make my life even more of a misery than it is already.

Rowan, age 13

Help, Cathy!
My life is not worth living. Yesterday, this girl who has been bullying me tore up my art project and threw my backpack into the school bins. She says if I tell

anyone, she'll beat me up and I believe her . . . so what am I supposed to do? Besides, who would believe me anyway?

Elena, age 12

Bullies don't want you to speak out. Why would they? It would get them into trouble, after all! So they tell you to keep quiet, or else things will get worse . . . Rowan and Elena are not the only victims afraid to speak out, but staying silent just protects the bully and allows her to go on tormenting you.

How can speaking out be worse than that?

The only way to stop bullying for good is to break the silence.

Yes, it's scary . . . but not as scary as allowing the bully to go on hurting you. If you want things to change, you must find the courage to speak out and get some help.

When bullying is this serious, staying silent is not an option.

Cathy

I told my mum I was being bullied at school and she wants to come in and talk to my teacher about it. Have I done the right thing?

Anna, age 10

Hi Cathy

I know I have to tell someone about what's happening at school, but who? I mentioned it to my form teacher a few weeks ago and he just said it would all blow over. I don't think the teachers really care.

Stella, age 12

Anna has done exactly the right thing. Telling someone about the bullying breaks the silence and gets some help on side.

Anna's mum knows she cannot sort things alone, so she plans to see the class teacher and take things one stage further – if Anna, her mum and teacher work together to stop the bullying, they have a very good chance of succeeding.

Stella has tried to speak out, but her class teacher didn't take her seriously. Stella must not give up. She could tell her guidance tutor or any sympathetic teacher, or see her year head, school counsellor or even her head teacher . . . and if she gets some backup from her family, things may move even faster towards sorting the problem out. On the whole, teachers really do care about the welfare of their students – that's why they became teachers, after all. Ask for help and you'll be given it . . . no school can afford to ignore bullying, and no student should ever have to live in fear.

Cathy
My class teacher and Head have promised me they can stop the bullying. I'm relieved I've told them, but scared too - what happens next?
                              Iris, age 13

Each school has its own way of dealing with bullies. Some will take a hard line, excluding the bullies and punishing them. Some have a gentler approach, with specially trained teachers who talk to bullies and victims and help them to work out solutions and new ways to behave. Some let other pupils show the bullies that pushing people around is not acceptable – circle time, golden time, bully courts and pupil meetings are all versions of this.

Whatever action your school takes, it should help to change things. If the bullying continues, tell your teacher – they cannot help unless they know the facts.

An End to Bullying

Dear Cathy
My sister was bullied for three years. The teachers didn't do anything to help and in the end she tried to hurt herself and ended up in hospital. She had to change schools. I'm telling you this because I've just read your book *Driftwood* and I know you'll understand. Bullying can ruin people's lives.

Mina, age 12

Hiya Cathy
I was bullied for a long time in primary and I didn't tell anyone about it. I lost all my confidence, and when I went to secondary school it started all over again. I changed schools and it still went on, and now I am home-educated, which is good, but I miss having friends. I don't think bullies even realize how much damage they do.

Victoria, age 13

Sometimes, things go wrong. Sometimes, for whatever reason, schools don't deal with things properly and the bullying continues. For Mina's sister, it all got too much to bear. She didn't know where else to turn for help, so she turned her anger and despair inwards, towards herself. Mina's sister is starting again in a new school, but I wonder if her tormentors have any idea how much pain they've caused her?

Victoria too has been let down by the system. Her confidence took so many knocks she became a permanent victim, always attracting the attention of the bullies no matter where she was. I hope that Victoria will use her time being home-schooled to rebuild her shattered self-esteem – there are lots of tips that could help Victoria in the next chapter.

Mina's sister and Victoria both felt very isolated and alone, but it doesn't have to be that way. There are many brilliant websites that focus on beating bullying, as well as helplines and support groups that can help victims and their families to overcome their problems and find a happier ending. If you are being bullied, or just feeling lost, hopeless or alone, you can always call ChildLine on 0800 1111. They will listen – and they can help.

Cathy

I have a terrible secret. Well, it's not even a secret — I am bullying a girl at school. She just really annoys me and she never stands up for herself, and it's just so easy to push her around and make her feel bad. I don't know why I do it, though, because my big brother treats me exactly the same way and I hate it. I just can't seem to help it.

Brittany, age 13

Hi Cathy

My friends have been acting more and more bitchy lately. They are bullying a new girl who happens to be a bit overweight, and making her life a misery. I try not to get involved, but I still feel bad because I'm not doing anything to stop it. I keep thinking that if I ignore it, they might just get bored and leave her alone.

Shaunie, age 14

What makes someone a bully? Often, like Brittany, they have been bullied themselves, perhaps at home. To them, making someone else feel small so that they can feel strong is a bit of a buzz. Brittany doesn't have any sympathy for her victim, yet she has a lot in common with her!

Shaunie isn't bullying anyone, but she feels very guilty because her friends are – and she isn't doing anything to stop them. Shaunie could talk to other girls in her group and see if any of them share her feelings – I bet a few of them are uncomfortable with what's happening. Together they can talk to the rest of the group and try to stop the bullying – or find new friends.

Many bullies are insecure, unhappy, selfish, lonely, angry . . . their own lives are empty, so they lash out at others to make themselves feel better. It doesn't take a genius to figure out that hurting other people isn't a great way to make yourself feel good! Bullying is not a great path to take through life. It won't win you friends, although plenty of people may be afraid of you. And if you go on pushing people around to get your own way, the chances are you'll end up in prison one day . . . seriously.

Like many bullies, Brittany needs help to find better ways to relate to people and better ways to feel confident – she can ask for help from her guidance teacher or school counsellor.

Bullying isn't good for anyone – the victim or the bully.

Cathy
I was bullied in my last school and it made me miserable. My new school has a fantastic anti-bullying policy, which makes all the difference – why can't all schools do this?
               Zakirah, age 11

Hey Cathy
My friend and I signed up to the Friendship Charter on your website. We'd like to help our school to be a bully-free zone.
Any ideas?
               Julia, age 13

All schools have to have an anti-bullying policy to protect students and ensure they have an education free from bullying. There are many ways of doing this, and some of the best ways allow the students to get involved too. After all, bullying is a problem for all of us – all of us can have a say in how to deal with it!

If you are worried about bullying, ask a sympathetic teacher to look at the issue with your class or year group. Together, you can come up with suggestions of ways to make bullying unacceptable in your school. No school ever has all the answers – there is always room for new ideas.

* Getting everyone involved in an anti-bullying policy helps – pupils, teachers, dinner ladies, janitors, playground supervisors, parents. Bullying affects us all.

* If bullying tends to happen in certain areas of the school or at certain times of day, teachers can keep a special eye on those areas.

* Buddies can be arranged to 'look out' for new pupils.

* A 'Bullying Box' can be set up in the school lobby where anonymous notes about bullying can be posted.

* 'Circle Time' can be used to discuss bullying behaviour and how to overcome it.

* Certain teachers and/or pupils can become anti-bullying counsellors, as

happens in the book *Driftwood* . . . victims can go to them in confidence and talk about their problems.

* Anti-bullying counsellors can help the bullies too, allowing them to talk about why they act the way they do and how they might change.

* The class can watch DVDs and read books about how bullying affects people, or listen to talks by those who have been victims in the past.

* Children can make posters, leaflets, stories and so on, explaining why bullying is not acceptable, helping the school management to draw up a firm set of guidelines for everyone to follow.

* Schools can sign up to the Cathy Cassidy Friendship Charter.

* Make it a basic rule that if anyone sees bullying taking place, they speak out – create zero tolerance for bullies.

Your ideas count, so get thinking – we're all in this together, and together we CAN stop bullying.

Helpbox

Read It . . .

* *Wise Guides: Bullying* by Michele Elliott (Hodder)
* *Don't Pick on Me* by Rosemary Stones (Piccadilly)
* *All About Bullying* by Lesley Ely (Hodder)

Websites:

www.childline.org.uk – sections on bullying, gangs

www.textsomeone.com – report bullying and get support by text

www.kidscape.org.uk/childrens/zap.html

www.beatbullying.org

www.bullybusters.org.uk

Helplines:

ChildLine – 0800 1111

Bullybusters – 0800 169 6928

Cathy's Books ... Published by Puffin

* *Driftwood* – how to help if a friend is being bullied . . .
* *GingerSnaps* – how it feels to be bullied and how to rebuild your confidence . . .

6. Confidence Tricks

This is probably the most important chapter in the book because if you don't have confidence in yourself, you're in big trouble! If you can't be your own best friend, how can you expect other people to like you? If you don't believe in yourself, how can you hope that others will?

Learning to like yourself, the good bits and the bad, is really important. Whether you want to make good friendships, have caring boyfriends, do well at school or follow your dreams and ambitions, you need self-esteem to do it! If you don't believe in yourself, you're more likely to give up when the going gets tough, telling yourself you 'just weren't good enough anyway'.

It's time to ditch the negative thoughts and learn how to think positive, in six simple steps. And don't be fooled by the title of this chapter . . . the tips that follow aren't tricks, they are techniques that really work!

Step One . . .

Accept Yourself!

Dear Cathy
I hate myself - I'm just so ugly. I suppose
you think I'm just feeling sorry for myself,
but I'm serious. I want a life!

Kira, age 13

Cathy
My friends are cool, clever and pretty
- I don't know why they put up with
me, really, because I'm none of those
things. Even my mum says I should try
to be more like my sisters ... I know
I'm a disappointment to her.

Sheridan, age 12.

If you don't like yourself, you will find it very
hard to reach your potential or find happiness
because every time life comes up with something
good, you'll find a way to mess it up. After all, you
don't deserve good things, do you? It's kind of a
vicious circle.

Kira and Sheridan need to see that they deserve friends, love, support and success just as much as anyone else. But first, they have to stop putting themselves down. Sheridan's problem could stem from her mum's comment – she needs to talk to her mum and clear the air. I'm pretty sure Sheridan's mum loves and values her daughter for who she is, and has no idea how much that one thoughtless comment, comparing Sheridan to her sisters, has dented her confidence. Sometimes, though, the people who are supposed to love and support us don't do such a great job of it, and that often leaves us struggling with low self-esteem.

That's tough, I know, but self-esteem is not about what other people think of you – it's about what YOU think. You can't buy self-esteem (I wish!) or get it from other people. If you only feel good when other people praise you or give you lots of attention, you're in trouble because no matter how many people you may seek approval from, the one that really matters is YOU.

I really identify with Kira's letter. At fourteen, I felt pretty much the same. I wasn't the most confident of teens, but I got by – until one day when I went shopping for a dress for a special party. I found a dress I loved, took it into the changing rooms, put it on and looked in the mirror . . . and my world fell apart.

The changing room had three walls of mirrors, so I could see myself all the way around rather than just face-on. I could see myself the way others could, and I was horrified. Sounds dramatic, but I was a pretty dramatic fourteen-year-old . . . and that was how I felt! I just couldn't believe I really looked like that.

What was wrong? I guess I just didn't like my profile, which showcased a nose that couldn't possibly have belonged to me . . . could it? The person in the mirror just wasn't ME.

I bought the dress, but I didn't get over that whole changing-room nightmare for years. I spent a decade avoiding angled mirrors and started wearing an elaborate hairstyle involving ponytails, backcombing and lots of scarves and ribbons to 'balance' my nose. I planned on getting a nose job as soon as I could scrape the cash together.

By the time I had a job and an income, though, I'd forgotten all about the nose-job plan. I'd just got used to the way I looked, learnt to like it, even. I was happy in my own skin. I still think I got the wrong nose somehow, but hey, I've learnt to live with it!

Learning to love the body we're in is one of the best favours we can do for ourselves. It may not be perfect, but so what? Work with it. Don't waste a decade, like I did, hung up on negative thoughts. Don't punish yourself with crash diets and dreams of plastic surgery – look in the mirror and smile . . . it's the first step to making friends.

Step Two . . .

Making Friends With You!

Look in the mirror and take a good look at that girl you see there . . . if she was a friend of yours, what would you say to her? What advice would you give her? Listen up, and act on it. Maybe she'd look cool with a new haircut, a sparkly lip gloss or just some concealer to zap those zits . . . there are lots more tips on making the best of yourself in the next chapter.

Before you leave that mirror, say something nice to the girl looking back at you, show her you think she's fab. Imagine you're complimenting a friend – you are, it's just that the friend is YOU!

Here are a few examples . . .

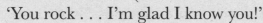

* 'You rock . . . I'm glad I know you!'
* 'You look great today!'
* 'You look really friendly and approachable when you smile!'
* 'You're really interesting and kind and quirky!'

It's weird at first, giving yourself compliments, but every positive message helps to raise your self-esteem!

....
: Step Three . . . :
....

Look for the Good Stuff! ❀ ❀ ❀

Dear Cathy

I know I am a let down to my family. I can't seem to do anything right. Once, when my mum was angry, she called me a sad little loser and sometimes I think that's exactly what I am . . .

Colette, age 13

Hello Cathy
My friend is always telling me
how stupid I am and how no
boys will ever like me. It gets me
down. If I'm so useless, what is
she doing hanging out with me?
                    Della, age 12

It hurts when people who are supposed to care about us put us down. If we are told often enough that we're stupid, useless or lacking in some way, slowly we come to believe it – it might be a parent, a teacher or a so-called 'friend' trampling all over our confidence, but the effect is the same. It hurts – and if it goes on, it wears down our self-esteem. Pretty soon, we can no longer see anything good about ourselves.

People who put others down to make themselves feel good are the ones with the problem. Colette's mum may simply have been very angry, but perhaps she is also bitter, resentful and depressed? Della's 'friend' enjoys making her mate feel bad, and that's a toxic kind of friendship – one Della needs to ditch, before it is too late.

It's fantastic when our friends, family and teachers boost our self-esteem and shine up our confidence with positive comments . . . but what if they don't? What if they chip away at us, piece by piece, trying to make us as unhappy as they are? It can be hard to stop that negative feedback seeping in and pulling us down.

That's why self-esteem has to start with YOU. It's no good just soaking up the nice/nasty things other people say. It's what you think that really matters.

So, back to the girl in the mirror . . . it's time to get to know her a bit better! Get yourself a sheet of paper and write down ten things you rate about yourself . . . yes, that's *rate*, not hate. We all have good qualities – it's time to uncover yours! If you're struggling, think about what you'd say to your new friend . . . what's cool, interesting and fun about her? Don't let her be shy . . . remind her of some of the things she's good at!

1   I love animals.
2   I'm good with little kids.
3   I'm a good listener.
4   I work hard in class.
5   I love reading.
6   I can keep a secret.

7 I make brilliant butterfly cakes!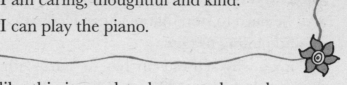
8 I'm quite tidy.
9 I am caring, thoughtful and kind.
10 I can play the piano.

A list like this is good to have on days when we are feeling negative . . . it shows us all the positive things we have to be glad about! Many negative things in life can be turned into positives . . . all you have to do is turn that frown upside down and look at things a different way.

When I was growing up, I read a book by Eleanor Porter about a girl called Pollyanna, who always looked on the bright side of things. Cheesy? Not so much – these days, governments employ experts to do exactly the same thing and call them 'spin doctors'. Spin doctors can't cure anything, but their job is to turn 'bad news' upside down and find the good in it . . . it's a cool trick. Try it!

* It's raining – but I can use my new *Hello Kitty* umbrella!

* I've got to wear glasses – but now I can see my crush better!

*   I messed up in my maths test – but now I know what I need to revise for next time!

Get Happy! 🌼🌼🌼🌼🌼🌼🌼🌼

Cathy

I feel so self-conscious, like everyone is watching me the whole time and expecting me to fall flat on my face. When you're shy, everything is such a struggle!

                    Keisha, age 12

Dear Cathy

My friends chat to a group of boys from the year above, but when I see them I panic and my words get tangled up and I wind up acting like a total idiot. I'm just an embarrassment!

                Abi, age 13

Keisha and Abi, I sympathize! I too was shy at school and boy did it make life difficult. Like Keisha, I always felt people were watching me, expecting me to slip up. Guess what . . . they weren't; they were way too busy worrying about their own problems to bother about me, but I didn't suss that until years later.

When you're shy, you assume the world revolves around YOU. It doesn't! What's the worst that can happen? You get your words mixed up or tell a joke that goes flat or trip in front of the coolest kids in the year . . . well, so what? You're human! It's allowed!

If I'd liked myself a little more back then, I might have been kinder to myself! If you're shy and self-conscious, you probably give yourself such a hard time you can hardly blame others if they sometimes join in. Time to change all that . . .

How do you remind yourself you're a gal worth knowing? Make a Happy Box! Find an old shoebox and decorate it with cut-out collage pics of your fave bands/actors/icons. Line the inside with fabric from a favourite old dress from when you were little. (Ask first . . . If your mum freaks because you've cut up her fave dress from your childhood, that Happy Box won't have got off to a great start!)

What goes in there?

* some glitter sprinkles, to give your life a little sparkle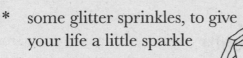
* your list of what's cool, fun and interesting about you
* a list of your role models (see chapter 7)
* special family photos/pics of best friends
* photos of happy moments/achievements, like when you were an angel in the infant school play; when you played recorder in assembly, aged eight; when you passed your Grade One ballet exam or held a cake sale to raise money for endangered species
* any *Pollyanna* thoughts you especially like
* a CD of your fave upbeat sounds . . . or childhood favourites
* certificates, letters, artwork, mascots, souvenirs and so on . . . even a scrap of tinsel from the Christmas tree or a painting of a purple spotted giraffe from Year Two

If it makes you smile, it can go in there!

Do it Anyway!

Hi Cathy
My English teacher has asked me to try out for the school play, and although part of me wants to, I'm scared I'd mess up and go bright red and everybody would laugh. I'd feel so stupid!

Jaime, age 13

Cathy
We have to give a speech in class and I'm dreading it. I just won't be able to get up in front of everyone like that without making an idiot of myself. It's my worst nightmare!

Olivia, age 12

Unless you're a drama diva, you probably don't like reading out in class, giving speeches or taking centre stage . . . but you know what? The times when you push yourself to go beyond what feels easy and comfortable are usually the times you achieve your best.

Take a peek into that Happy Box. Remember how nervous you were playing recorder in assembly? Remember how your heart raced and your mind went blank, the day of that ballet exam? Yet you survived, and now you can be proud of your achievements. It takes courage to admit you're scared and then go ahead and do the thing that scares you anyway, but it's a part of growing up.

If we run away from every challenge, we never learn.

When I realized that being a writer wasn't just about daydreaming and writing down the dreams, I was pretty amazed. Apparently, being a children's writer these days means going out and about, meeting and talking to readers in schools, libraries and book festivals far and wide. I didn't like the sound of that, to start with. Talking to big groups of kids . . . about me? That was never part of the plan! I didn't have much of a choice, so I did it anyway.

It was like giving a speech at school, only about a million times scarier, but I survived, and soon found I enjoyed the buzz and the feedback. These days, it's one of my favourite parts about being a writer – meeting you, the readers!

So, Jaime, if you try out for the school play you might not be perfect. Better not try, huh? And Olivia, safer not to face those fears about public speaking . . . best throw a sicky that day and wriggle out of it. But who would you be cheating? Yourself.

Jaime's teacher believes she'd be great in the play – and she could be, if she just gives herself a chance. Many actors/actresses describe themselves as shy – but by 'becoming' someone else when acting in a play, they step outside that shyness and learn to shine.

Olivia's confidence will take yet another knock if she runs away from this challenge. The way forward is to choose a subject she really cares about and research it well . . . she may still feel shaky on the day, but 'acting' confident will get her through.

Here's the most powerful confidence 'trick' of all. When you have to do something you really, really don't want to do, fix a smile on your face, admit no fear and pretend you're coping . . . and do it anyway. You might even fool yourself . . . and you'll have proved you have the courage to face down your fears. The next time, it won't be quite as scary. Promise!

Step Six . . .

Get Lucky! ❀❀❀❀❀❀❀❀❀❀

Cathy
My best friend has a really nice house and a lovely family and plenty of money. She's pretty and clever and popular and always happy . . . she's so lucky, it's not fair!

Rashida, age 11

Dear Cathy
I was bullied when I was younger and used to be very unhappy. With the help of a great teacher and some good friends, I have turned things around and now I feel lucky those things happened as they taught me so much. I think I see the same message in your books. We only have one life – we owe it to ourselves to make the most of it!

Cassie, age 14

Cassie's letter says it all . . . you only have one life, so make the most of it! The way you choose to see things can make a huge difference to the life you have, but remember, it IS your choice!

Remember the jealousy monster we mentioned back in the Friendship chapter? Here it goes again . . . causing a whole bunch of trouble. Rashida sees herself as unlucky and her friend as lucky. Well, the mind is a powerful thing, and if you genuinely believe you are lucky you will attract good luck to yourself. When new things happen you'll tend to see them as lucky too – it's about having a positive attitude.

Imagine that Rashida and her 'lucky' friend find a purse containing fifty pounds, hand the purse in to the police station and later are given a reward of five pounds for their honesty. Rashida might see that as 'unlucky' – just five pounds? Not enough! Rashida's friend would look on the bright side, happy to have five pounds she didn't have before, and to have found the purse and returned it to its rightful owner.

Being lucky or unlucky – it's all about attitude. It's a choice you make. I'd rather be lucky . . . how about you?

As Cassie says, life is for living . . . so make every minute count!

* Always wanted to try a new hobby/ interest? Sign up, today!

* Try a karate class – great for confidence boosting!

* Learn a new skill/language/ musical instrument!

* Join a youth club/ drama group and meet new people.

* Help out at the local retirement home/ animal sanctuary.

* Make a list of things you'd like to do before the year is out – then start making it happen!

* Take regular exercise.

* Eat healthy foods!

* Do something that relaxes you, like yoga or meditation.

* Hang out with friends who make you feel good about yourself.

* Have fun, study hard, and do one random act of kindness every day!

What's with the random-acts-of-kindness thing? They're something my character Sam Taylor talks about in *GingerSnaps* . . . things like helping out a new kid at school, sending a letter/email to an old friend or even just walking the dog! The world needs more random acts of kindness, and the best thing of all is, they make YOU feel good too.

What goes around comes around. If you put good stuff out into the world, good stuff will come back to you. If you put bad stuff out, bad stuff will come back to you.

Write a list of random acts of kindness you could try on others . . . everything from doing the washing-up or cleaning your dad's car to helping a new Year Seven/student teacher. Add the list to your Happy Box – doing something for others is a perfect antidote to feeling sorry for yourself.

What else can go in your Happy Box? A set of 'treat' cards to cheer you up on bad days, maybe . . . cards that give you permission to do something fun, like take a long bubble bath, have a mani/pedicure, a girls' night in with slushy DVDs . . . you decide!

When you're feeling low, your Happy Box can remind you of the good times, the things you've achieved, the things you plan to achieve.

Oh, and the next time you see the girl in the mirror, say hi to her from me . . . she's cool!

Helpbox

Read It . . .
* *Think Pink* by Lisa Clark (Macmillan) – has a fab section of self-esteem
* *Wise Guides: Self-Esteem* by Anita Naik (Hodder)
* *Seven Day Self-Esteem Super Booster* by Jenny Alexander (Hodder)

Cathy's Books . . . Published by Puffin
* *GingerSnaps* – lacking confidence, being yourself, Sam Taylor and the random acts of kindness . . .
* *Driftwood* – feeling invisible, not fitting in
* *Sundae Girl* – feeling shy/embarrassed

7. Being Yourself

Well, who else are you going to be? Hmmm. For some of us, growing up is not about discovering our own unique style, but more about following the crowd, fitting in and trying to be just like everyone else. Why? Because that way, you won't attract attention or risk being teased, misunderstood or laughed at for being different.

Well, maybe.

We all want to be liked, and we all want to make the best of ourselves, but style and fashion and what you believe in are very personal things. It's OK to be different. It's OK to be you!

Who Am I?

Dear Cathy
Ever since I was very small I've had this strange idea that I must have been switched at birth, that I'm not actually a part of the family I grew up in. I'm not trying to say I'm a princess or a gypsy or the secret daughter of a tragic movie star . . . just that I've never felt like I belonged!

Deborah, age 13

Growing up is not a picnic. It can be an uncomfortable time, and there are no guarantees your family will understand what you are going through or know how exactly to support you. Sometimes, like Deborah, you may feel like an alien who landed up on Planet Earth completely by accident! I felt this way for quite a while as a teenager.

Like Deborah, my life was not a cute teen novel either. No secret message arrived to tell me I had been given a scholarship to Hogwarts School of Witchcraft and Wizardry or had suddenly inherited the crown of a small European country. I was stuck at home with kind, well-meaning parents, an annoying little brother (actually he was sweet, but I didn't always appreciate him) and a bunch of friends who just didn't understand me.

Nobody understood me. I didn't even understand myself!

I escaped into books and the pages of my favourite teen mag, where life always seemed glam, cool and exciting, and sensitive, drop-dead gorgeous boys were never in short supply. I dreamt a lot.

I guess that being a moody, misunderstood and dreamy teenager may have been great practice for becoming an author, but it didn't make for a whole lot of fun at the time. Maybe I just worried too much. Feeling like an alien/outsider/weirdo is normal when you're growing up . . . sometimes, anyhow!

In the end, I realized I probably hadn't been abandoned on my parents' doorstep as a child. I was a mixture of my shy, kind, anxious mum and dreamy, eccentric, hard-working dad, with shades of my fun-loving little brother stirred in for variety, and a whole raft of extra ingredients that were all down to ME.

If you don't quite see how you fit into your family yet, hang on . . . the chances are you will!

Dear Cathy

Were you ever a tomboy? I am. I just want to be me, but some of the girls think I'm weird. I don't understand why style has to be such a big issue!

Jayne, age 12

Hey Cathy

I hope it's OK for me to write to you,
being a boy and everything. I do love your
books! People label me as a geek and that
really annoys me. I enjoy school, and I
have big ambitions, but I have feelings
too! I hate being made to feel like an
oddball just because I happen to work
hard.

　　　Martin, age 11

Some of us make a choice to be ourselves, no
matter what . . . and some of us just can't help
it. We stand out from the crowd because we do
things our way – we're different. Other people may
not always know what to make of individuals like
Jayne and Martin, but so what? They are true to
themselves and happy in their own skin, and that's
what counts.

It's not fair that anyone gets labelled with tags
they'd rather not have, but if this has happened to
you, remember that people aren't necessarily trying
to hurt you, just work you out. You can always re-
label yourself as something you DO like the sound
of! It takes all sorts to make a world, and if Jayne
and Martin get to know some of the kids who don't

know what to make of them right now, there might be surprises on both sides . . .

Don't judge by appearances – you could be missing out on a bunch of cool new friends.

Style Matters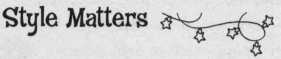

Hi Cathy
There's a girl in my school who wears weird shoes and clothes and listens to bands most people have never heard of. I like some of the music she does, and I really, really admire her for being true to herself! I wish I could be!

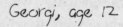
Georgi, age 12

Dear Cathy
Our friend has gone all 'emo' over the summer holiday. She listens to loud, miserable bands and has dyed her hair black (it was a really nice blondie-brown before). What if she gets really depressed and starts to self-harm or something? How can we help her?

Hollie & Nia, age 11

Cathy

I wish I could be like Joey from *Driftwood*
and really express myself in the clothes
I wear. I love putting new looks together
from charity shop finds, but I don't
think my friends would approve!

Ella, age 12

Georgi is starting to see that there's something exciting and empowering about being your own person. The girl she admires doesn't struggle to fit in with a particular crowd, she just does things her own way. Her clothes and music express who she is, rather than just reflecting the latest trends. She's a real individual!

For Georgi, that seems wonderful, but out of reach. Perhaps she doesn't yet know herself well enough to put across this kind of strong image, or maybe she just lacks the confidence? Growing up is a voyage of discovery, and we learn more about ourselves, our likes and dislikes, who we really are, every day. Georgi might like to try to make friends with the girl she admires . . . they may have a lot more in common than just music!

Hollie and Nia are confused. Their friend has changed, and they don't understand why or how – they just want things to go back to the way they were. Their friend has found a style that she loves, music that means something to her, even a haircut that feels 'right'. She has taken control of her life and made some strong style statements, and she is happy with that.

Perhaps she feels that black hair is more 'her' than blondie-brown? That listening to emotional music helps her to feel understood, not depressed? That being 'emo' is just a part of who she is? The only problem she has is that her friends Hollie and Nia don't understand this! All that black, all those loud, dramatic bands and the crazy stuff some newspapers have written about emos are all worrying Hollie and Nia.

If they have reason to believe their friend is depressed or self-harming, they should tell a trusted teacher at once. If not, they should calm down and try talking to her, find out more about her style, her music and how she is feeling. If she is down, the chances are it's because her best friends are treating her as a stranger – she is still the same person underneath!

Ella is not alone – many young people use clothes as a way to express who they are. A pair of trainers, a back-combed quiff, a bright vest top or a style of jacket can all give clues about our likes, dislikes, musical tastes, style. Sometimes, our clothes help us to fit into a friendship group, become part  of a 'tribe', and at other times mark us out as 'different'.

Ella knows she wants to try out some new looks, but worries about what her friends will say. They may not understand or approve, but they'll still accept her style choices! If expressing yourself through clothes is important to you, you may find you have to go ahead anyway . . . being just like everybody else is not an option!

Like Ella, when I was younger, I was too worried to dress the way I really wanted to . . . but when I did start sneaking weird and wonderful items into my wardrobe, it felt great! My friends took it in their stride and it felt natural to show my creative side in the way I dressed . . . I went from super-shy to quietly confident almost overnight.

So what if people were looking at me? Suddenly, that was my choice – I could turn heads with a crazy vintage dress, Doc Marten boots and through-a-hedge-backwards hair and still keep smiling. Because that was the way I WANTED to look. That was ME.

I don't dress like that any more, but I don't follow fashion, either . . . I stick to my own style. It's a little bit weird and wacky, just like me . . . and that's the way I like it!

Let It Out ❀ ❀ ❀ ❀ ❀ ❀ ❀ ❀

Cathy

I have a great group of friends who are very caring and lots of fun – quite 'girly' girls. I am like them in many ways, but I also have some very strong views about animal cruelty, endangered species and eating meat. I'd like to talk about these things sometimes, but I'm worried they'll think I'm a freak!

Sita, age 13

Dear Cathy

My friends are mostly great, but one does make racist comments sometimes and nobody ever says anything to her. I am mixed race, although you might not think so to look at me, but I think I'd find it upsetting no matter what. I just cannot

stand prejudice and ignorance. What
would you do?
Fern, age 14

Standing up for what you believe in – that's a
tough one. We all know we should do it, but finding
the courage can take time. If you have strong
views, like Sita, but usually keep them to yourself,
your friends won't be expecting you to suddenly
steer the conversation away from nail varnish
and boy bands towards more serious topics. They
might raise an eyebrow, but I bet they'd be quite
interested to hear your ideas and feelings . . . try it
and see!

Sita may find that some of her friends feel the
same way. Together, they may agree to cut down on
meat or even go veggie, or check that their make-up
brands are not tested on animals . . . even raise money
to save African elephants! Even if Sita's friends don't
share her views, it's good to talk about issues like this
sometimes . . . there's more to life than nail varnish.
And friends can have different views, as long as they
still respect each other.

Fern's dilemma is even more clear-cut. She has
strong views on racism – hearing racist comments
makes her skin crawl. Most of us would feel exactly
the same way, but how do you tell a friend they

are seriously out of order? It's not easy.

When you bite back your feelings to keep the peace, it feels bad. Fern needs to tell her friend how much the racism upsets her and why it is unacceptable. Sometimes, we hear something shocking and let it go because we can't quite believe we really heard it – we don't want to believe a friend could think such a thing. The problem with that is, it passes on a message that prejudice and racism is OK, and that's *not* the case – ever.

Fern may not want to be the one to stand up and speak out about this, but unless she faces the comments head-on and tells her friend just what she thinks, she'll go on feeling bad inside. Hopefully, if she speaks out, her friends will also find the courage to say what they think, and the racist comments will stop. Fern's friend may question her own attitudes, and change the way she thinks . . . but if not, then at least she'll know how ugly and ignorant her comments seem to others.

Sometimes, you just have to stand up and be counted. This takes courage, of course, but it feels a whole lot better than staying silent! If you have strong feelings, don't keep them to yourself – they are a part of you, so don't be ashamed of your opinions and passions. And if you see injustice or intolerance, speak out against it . . . someone has to.

Peer Pressure ❀❀❀❀❀❀❀

Help, Cathy!
My friend has started smoking and is trying to get me to try it too. I really don't want to, but I don't want to lose her.
Carrie, age 13

Cathy
My friends have got into a habit of hanging out in the park after school with some boys from the year above us. So far I've gone along with it, but it can get very flirty and rowdy and once one of the boys had some cider too. I feel really out of my depth.
Kristi, age 13

When your friends try to get you to join in with something you really don't want to, that's peer pressure. It's hard to resist because you want to please your friends, yet it feels uncomfortable too, because whatever they are suggesting just isn't right for you. You can feel it. You know it. Yet saying no . . . well, it's hard.

Carrie doesn't want to start smoking. She knows the habit is expensive, addictive, uncool and seriously bad for her health and looks. But still, she doesn't want to lose her friend. The irony is that Carrie's friend may have exactly the same reasons for wanting her to start smoking too . . . she feels a bit scared and out of her depth with the habit, and knows that if she can draw Carrie in as well she'll feel safer, more secure. Double the reason, really, for saying no!

Like Carrie, Kristi feels that if she stops doing what her friends want after school, she may lose them. At the moment, it's just that she isn't that interested in hanging out with a bunch of loud and lairy lads, but also that she can see where things are heading . . . and that's not what she wants. If something is wrong for you, it's wrong, no matter who asks you to do it . . . both Carrie and Kristi have to step back from the pressure and say no.

Perhaps Carrie's friend will sulk and go on smoking, or perhaps she'll give up. Perhaps Kristi's friends will call her a baby and drift away a little, hanging out more and more with the boys, but perhaps some will agree with Kristi and choose to back off a little. Standing up to peer pressure is a risk because you never know for sure how the other person will react. It's still a risk you have to take, though, to do the right thing for you.

Carrie and Kristi should read through the chapter on Confidence Tricks so they are feeling strong inside. If they like and respect themselves, they will no longer do things that make them feel uncomfortable. Kids who lack self-esteem and do not feel happy inside often find themselves in trouble, or in difficult or dangerous situations . . . because they are scared to say 'no'.

Why is saying 'no' so tough? It's such a little word, but a powerful one. If you let your mates call the shots and sometimes find yourself doing things you'd rather not, practise saying 'no' a little more often. A true friend will respect you for that.

Role Models

Cathy
I get so depressed sometimes when I compare myself to my mates, or, worse, to the models in my sister's fashion mags. How can I stop feeling this way?

Ruby, age 12

Ruby and Jenna need to stop comparing themselves with others. It's easy to look at others and imagine that they're confident and sussed, but maybe they have doubts and worries too. If they are genuinely confident, try learning from them. Confident people are positive, upbeat and look on the bright side. They don't put themselves – or others – down. They have a 'can-do' attitude and a real enthusiasm for life. Don't envy them, try acting like them!

Comparing yourself to fashion mag models is especially bad news. Ruby needs to remember that fashion mag shots are often airbrushed to get rid of blotchy skin and extra pounds – and that's *after* the models have had a professional make-up job. They may look good, but that's their job, remember! For some fashion models, the pressures to be thin are so great that they become borderline anorexic. Good role models? No way!

A good role model is someone you can learn from. You may not want to be exactly like them, but there are things about them you admire. Here are some of mine . . .

* **my dad**
* **Rebecca Adlington**, Olympic gold medallist and record breaker, and **Eleanor Simmonds**, at thirteen, the UK's youngest ever individual Paralympic gold medallist
* **Kimya Dawson**, punk/folk singer who refuses to be pigeonholed (check her out on the soundtrack from the movie *Juno*)
* **Nelson Mandela**, campaigner against racial segregation in South Africa, who was sent to prison for twenty-seven years for his beliefs. Mandela went on to become president of South Africa and was given the Nobel Peace Prize in 1993
* **Bob Geldof**, punk singer, creator of Band Aid and campaigner against famine, poverty and Third World debt

There are lots of other people I admire too . . . from Barack Obama to some of my best friends. Some people are just inspiring! When readers tell me that I am their role model, I feel very honoured. I know most of those girls won't grow up to be writers, but if they dare to dream and make just some of those dreams come true, that's brilliant!

Look around and choose some good role models for yourself, people you can learn from. Decide what you admire about them and why. You can even stick their pics on to card and slip them into your Happy Box from the last chapter to look at whenever you need inspiration!

Being Different

Dear Cathy

I have had epilepsy since I was small. I have to take medication to control it, which does work most of the time, but I live in fear of having a seizure in front of my new high-school friends. I just want to be normal!

Lydia, age 11

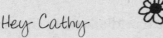

Hey Cathy

I have a disability and need to use a
wheelchair. I have a group of brilliant
mates who have stuck by me since junior
school, but lately I can't help but notice
how strangers see me. It's like they pity
me . . . or else they look right through me
as if I'm not there at all. How can I show
them I am every bit as good as they are?
It makes me so sad.

Harley, age 12

Lydia and Harley are both struggling with physical problems, but coping very differently. Lydia's epilepsy is mostly invisible, as the medication she takes is keeping it under control. She has chosen not to tell her friends, as she so badly wants to be like everybody else, but hiding a serious condition like epilepsy is not a good plan. If Lydia does have a seizure, her friends may be shocked and frightened – and they won't know how best to help her.

It may feel risky, but Lydia needs to open up to her new friends and tell them about her condition

. . . it's part of trusting them, and allowing them to be true, supportive friends. The more Lydia trusts her friends to know about her condition and be there for her, the more chance she has of living her life to the full . . . of being 'normal'. Believe it or not, though, there IS no 'normal' – we are all individuals, unique, often imperfect, but doing our best. That's about as normal as it gets!

Harley's disability is more visible, and her problem is not telling others about it, but handling the way some people judge her. Her friends know the real Harley, but strangers may make assumptions – because of the wheelchair – that have nothing to do with reality.

The message here is to always look at the person and not the disability. Harley is a lively girl with strong views and plenty of confidence . . . she's proof that a physical disability doesn't have to stand in your way. She knows that she's as good as anyone. Hopefully, once they get to know her, others will get the message too.

There's No Such Thing as Perfect ✽

Hey Cathy
I am part of a really cool crowd

at school, which is what I always wanted. I should be happy, but it's not as good as I thought it would be. I miss my old friends and sometimes I am just plain bored. I have recently read *GingerSnaps* and I really connected with the story because I think what you are saying is, popularity isn't as important as you think. Well, I think I am starting to agree.

Margaret, age 12

Dear Cathy

People say I have it all - looks, brains, popularity - yet I feel like something's missing, but I just don't know what. I feel like I'm just playing a part, pretending, and that if my friends see that they won't want to know me. I don't even know who I am any more! And I hate all this pressure

to be perfect because I don't think
I can keep it up for much longer.
                    Mikki, age 14

Being popular . . . it's something many of us dream of, but what does it actually mean? To be in with the cool crowd, the popular crew, the golden kids . . . the ones the whole school admire . . . surely, that would be something?

Being popular is just another label, and one you have to work pretty hard to keep up with. Margaret has discovered that 'being popular' is not as exciting as she imagined. She misses her old friends who may not have been 'popular', but were probably a whole lot more caring/interesting/fun. Margaret may not stay with the 'cool' kids for much longer – she isn't happy, and eventually I think she will choose real friendship over popularity.

For Mikki, the struggle of trying so hard to fit in is wearing thin. She has been playing a part for so long she has lost sight of who she really is. Mikki can work on her confidence and self-esteem, since it seems that beneath the surface it's nowhere near as strong as it may look from the outside. Using the tips and tricks in the last chapter, she can work on liking and accepting

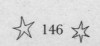

herself – the real Mikki, the person behind the 'perfect' mask. People who don't like themselves or have strong self-esteem can often find themselves hiding behind a 'fake' image or putting up with friends and situations that are not good for them.

Being perfect . . . it's an act nobody can keep up forever, and Mikki doesn't have to. It's OK to be real, with mixed-up feelings and happy and sad days. It's OK to have days when you don't want to spend three hours straightening your hair and painting your nails, days when you'd rather slob out in skinny jeans than totter around in skyscraper heels. It's OK if you get a 'B' or 'C' grade now and again, instead of all 'A's. It's OK if you want to eat apple pie instead of salad, or help behind the scenes in the school play instead of stressing about whether you'll land the lead role. It's OK to fancy the quiet boy with the specs who sits in front of you in science rather than the flashy boy who captains the footy team, but never talks about anything except himself.

In a word, it's OK to be YOU.

In fact, it's essential . . . you're the one person you cannot hide from, and if you try to be something you're not you will make yourself unhappy pretty fast.

Helpbox

Read It . . .

* *BeautyLicious* by Lisa Clark (Macmillan) – my fave girly style bible
* *Growing Up with Diabetes* by Alicia McAuliffe
* *Epilepsy: The Ultimate Teen Guide* by Kathlyn Gay (Scarecrow Press)
* *Do the Right Thing – A Teenager's Guide to Surviving Any Social Situation* by Jane Goldman (Piccadilly)
* *How 2 B Happy* by Jenny Alexander (A & C Black)

Websites:

www.childline.org.uk – sections on how you look, peer pressure

www.childrenfirst.nhs.uk – teen and kids' sections with tons of info on health worries, families, feelings and more

Cathy's Books . . . Published by Puffin

* *GingerSnaps* – being true to yourself, not allowing yourself to be pushed around

8. Dream On

Some of us are natural dreamers. We're talented at it, we have a skill. We dream at home. We dream at school, when we should be concentrating on equilateral triangles and the life cycle of the frog. We could pass exams in dreaming, getting A grades and merits effortlessly. We just can't help it.

Not everyone is a natural dreamer, but most of us start out that way. Our minds like telling stories or jumping off at tangents, painting pictures or creating crazy scenes. Dreaming is cool.

The biggest problem with dreaming is that a lot of the time, adults just don't appreciate it. They are likely to get annoyed if you are dreaming when you should be eating your dinner or tidying your room or learning French vocabulary. (Dream = *rêve*, in case your teacher asks!)

Adults sometimes tell you that dreaming is a BAD thing. They will tell you that dreaming is a waste of time, a skive.

My message is . . . DON'T LISTEN!!!!

Dreaming is not bad. Dreaming is good, better than hot chocolate fudge cake in fact, and not many things in this life are better than that.

Dreaming is the most powerful kind of magic we have for making things happen. How? Well, you can dream up a story and then write it down, but that's not really what I mean. I'm talking about dreams that focus on the future, dreams of things you'd like to be, things you'd like to achieve . . . a dream like that is special.

And if you can dream it, you can do it!

Big Ideas

Hi Cathy
I want to be an actress one day.
My mum says I should go for it, but my dad says I need to get a real job because people like me don't get to do things like that. How can I show him he's wrong?
Gwen, age 10

Dear Cathy
I would like to be a doctor and find a cure for cancer. It means a lot to me because my grandad died of cancer, but it's not a dream I can really talk about because I don't think other people would get it.
Eden, age 12

Gwen and Eden understand the magic of dreams. They both have a goal, a picture of what they want to do one day, and they believe in that dream. They know that other people's doubts or disbelief can shake the dream, so they stay silent about their hopes and ambitions unless they are with someone they know will be supportive.

Gwen's dad doesn't mean to be unsupportive, but he is worried that acting could be a very difficult career for her, and doesn't want her to be disappointed. He's right, she has set herself a very tough challenge, but she is determined . . . and that kind of determination should be encouraged. Yes, Gwen should work hard at school, keep her options open and pass as many exams as she can. But she could also look at drama groups or classes, which would help her to see whether she has a skill for the career she's dreaming of.

Eden's dream is lovely, but even more ambitious! I suspect her friends *would* admire her motives and be supportive, but sometimes keeping a dream secret can make it even more special.

Eden and Gwen may find that no matter how hard they work, dreams don't always work out exactly as they imagine. Gwen may not become a famous movie star, but perhaps a TV actress, a drama teacher or even an accountant who takes the lead role in the local amateur dramatics production every Christmas . . . but she will have followed her dream, and that will make her happy. Eden may not discover a cure for cancer, but perhaps she'll become a doctor or nurse working with cancer patients, or a research scientist working on new medicines and treatments. I think she'd be happy with those versions of the dream too!

Fame at Last

Cathy
I want to be famous. I look at programmes like *Big Brother* and *The X Factor* and know that it will be my turn one day. I want it so much I just know it has to happen!
Cordie, age 12

Dear Cathy
I want to be rich and famous just like you. Do you live in a mansion? Do you know lots of stars? Did you always want to be famous?
Linda, age 10

Cordie and Linda have big dreams too, but they're not as likely to bring happiness and fulfilment. Wishing to be an actress or a doctor is one thing, but wishing to be famous? Well, be careful what you wish for!

Most people who become famous work VERY hard to earn their fame, but usually they are not seeking fame itself. They just want to do well in their chosen career!

If you want to be famous, ask yourself why. If you are dreaming of a day when you'll be adored by millions and have everything you could wish for, it could be that you need to work on your self-esteem because fame really isn't a magic cure that will make you happier. If you are looking for love or attention or happiness, you really need to find those things closer to home. Check out the Confidence Tricks chapter again, and make friends with that girl in the mirror . . . if you have strong self-esteem, you don't need millions of others to make you feel good about yourself.

Fame is not a career or even a lifestyle. An artist called Andy Warhol once said, 'everyone will be famous for fifteen minutes' and he had a point, with shows like *Big Brother* where people can become famous (and rich!) just for being mean, or rude, or ditzy, or even just wearing very short skirts! Fame like that doesn't last and leaves you wanting more, a little like a spoilt toddler who wants more toys, more attention, more fuss.

Wanting to be rich and famous without putting the work in first is a bit like wanting to eat your pudding without having any main course . . . or wanting presents every day of the year, whether it's your birthday/Christmas or not. For what it's worth, it is very hard to handle fame – harder still when you are very young.

Many young stars go badly off the rails because they cannot cope with the media attention, the intrusion, the stress, the pressure. They starve themselves to avoid being called chubby, use drink or drugs to block out reality, hook up with unsuitable friends and lovers, are often very lonely . . . they are like a car crash just waiting to happen.

Does this sound like a happy life?

Cordie would be better off finding a dream that might be a little more rewarding – not in terms of money or fame, but satisfaction, achievement, happiness. As for Linda, well, she is not the only one to assume that all writers are rich and famous . . . but I don't know one fellow writer who drives a Rolls-Royce, lives in a castle, or gets mobbed for autographs every time they leave the house. There may be one or two out there, but even if that's so,

I guarantee they didn't start writing for the cash or the kudos!

Most of the time, fame and riches are a reward for hard work. If these things matter to you, then sure, build them into your dream, but don't make them an end in themselves . . . that way disaster lies.

Making It Happen

Dear Cathy
I want to be a writer when I grow up. Can you tell me what exams I need and what I should study at university?
            Rupa, age 13

Hey Cathy
I want to be a graphic designer. It's my dream, but I am not the best in my class at art and get better marks at French and music. Sometimes, I worry that I am kidding myself.
            Libby, age 14

Rupa has worked out that if you have a plan, you have a better chance than ever of making your wish come true. She is gathering in all the information she needs to make her dream a reality . . . if you don't ask, you don't learn.

My answer to Rupa was to work hard at English and at all of her subjects – a good general knowledge is helpful for any writer. Some writers study English or Creative Writing at university, but many don't. I went to art college and studied illustration! It didn't matter – what made me a writer was the fact that I loved to write, always. It was just a part of me. I practised all the time, and eventually found a job in journalism, later freelanced and finally started writing books . . . but every writer has a different story.

Some never go to university at all . . . they just live a vivid, adventurous life and use all of that life experience to feed their work. Sometimes, there are no right or wrong ways! Whichever path Rupa chooses, I think she will do well because she is looking ahead, making plans, taking steps to make the dream real.

Libby's letter struck home because I had just the same dilemma at fourteen. I loved art as much as writing, and longed to be an artist, but I worried that I wasn't good enough. Perhaps I wasn't, but I wanted to be – badly. I worked really hard and

 got myself to art college and scraped a living for years as an illustrator, fitting it in around my magazine work. I pushed the talent I had to the max, because I wanted to succeed.

Sometimes, people will tell you that you don't have what it takes for a certain career. You can accept the advice and watch your dreams and confidence fizzle, or use it to spur you on. Best of all, perhaps, you can adjust your dream, and turn it into something with more chance of success . . . Libby can find out all she can about careers in graphic design, visit art colleges, talk to tutors and students. Like Rupa, she can start planning, researching, gathering information . . . preparing to succeed.

But dreams alone are not enough.

Cathy
I want to be a fashion designer. It's my dream, and I have taught myself to sew and I love turning old stuff into something new and different. I am studying art, but our school doesn't have a textiles option - will this matter?   Tira, age 14

Hello Cathy

My dream is to be a dancer. I do ballet, modern and tap twice a week and have done for years. My plan is to study dance at a performing arts college, but my little sister has started saying only one or two people ever make it as dancers and I may as well not bother. It really gets to me.   Aimee, age 13

Following your dreams is one thing . . . and don't get me wrong, it's a big thing! But you need to do more than just follow – you need to grab those dreams and work hard to make them happen. One thing is for certain: they won't come true all by themselves!

Tira has the right idea. She isn't waiting for anyone to tell her what to do . . . she's working it out right now. Already, she is thinking like a fashion designer, learning basic skills. Studying art at GCSE and A level (or Standard Grade/Intermediate Two/Higher, if you are in Scotland) is important to strengthen skills in drawing, painting and colour.

Tira may have enjoyed a textiles course, but it is not essential for admission to a fashion degree – most unis will be way more interested to see the designs and pieces she has created herself. A passion for your chosen career counts for a lot.

Aimee is also determined to make her dream happen. She has worked very hard over many years, and has researched and planned what happens next, but her sister's words have hit home. Negative comments can make us doubt ourselves, but it's likely that Aimee's sister is a little envious of her sister's talents. Very few dancers become famous names, but there are many who quietly make a living doing what they love. And as I've said, there are jobs in all kinds of related areas too, from teaching to choreography . . . Aimee has plenty of options.

If you are following a dream, you have to believe in it – and in yourself!

Cathy
A boy in my class has been offered work experience at the local TV studios because one of the producers is his uncle. I am so annoyed because this would be my dream, and he isn't

even bothered about it!

Kauther, age 14

Dear Cathy

I'd love to be a singer-songwriter, and for the last year I've been in a band with some kids from school. I've written a lot of songs, sent off tons of demo CDs and posted clips on *YouTube*. We have our own website, and we've had a couple of gigs at the school, which have been good practice. We've just been asked to play our first festival — so you see dreams can come true!

Andie, age 15

We talked about this a bit in the Confidence Tricks chapter. Some people are luckier than others . . . or are they? Kauther is upset because a friend has the work experience she'd have loved, but did she think of approaching the TV studio herself or doing anything to arrange something similar?

You can wait a very long time for someone to offer you your dream on a plate. The chances are, it won't happen – we make our own luck.

Andie's letter shows that hard work and

determination really do pay off. What do successful people from all walks of life have in common? They work a whole lot harder than the average person! To be really, really good at anything, you have to put in the practice – lots of it. Every day, for weeks, months, years. It has to be your passion, your love.

And when you are really good at what you do, you have to take things a step further and create some opportunities, as Andie has done. Don't wait for fate to tap you on the shoulder – be lucky!

So . . . the bottom line is, it's OK to dream. Dreaming is what lifts us up above all the ordinary, humdrum stuff – it gives us something to aim for, something to work for. It's a little bit of magic in our everyday lives because it's the way we begin to create our future.

Don't ever let anyone tell you that dreaming is a waste of time . . . dare to dream, and dream big. Then follow that dream, and work hard to make it happen! There are no guarantees, but if it's something that matters to you, you'll never regret going after it.

And sometimes, if you're lucky, dreams really can come true.

Helpbox

Read It . . .

* *How to be a Pop Star* by David Orme (Trailblazers)
* *Careers Uncovered: Art and Design* by Emma Caprez (Trotman)
* *Careers Uncovered: Performing Arts* by Dee Pilgrim (Trotman)
* *How to be a Brilliant Writer* by Jenny Alexander (A & C Black)

Read It . . .

www.stagecoach.co.uk – part-time theatre arts schools for children/teens with an interest in acting/dancing/singing

www.themusicplace.co.uk – inspirational learning/summer schools for all aspects of music

www.connexions-direct.com – choosing Year Nine options, quizzes, info on career choices

www.kidzworld.com – check out the WORK IT section for a cool careers quiz

9. Family Matters

When I was little, our school reading books had bright, pretty pics of the perfect family inside. The dad always wore a suit, drove a shiny car and raked the leaves in the garden on a Sunday, wearing a hand-knitted cardigan. The mum wore a checked apron and red lipstick, and baked cakes and arranged flowers, while looking calm and serene. The brothers and sisters were always neatly turned out, polite and smiling. Even the dog and the cat were too good to be true.

Life wasn't like that for me. My dad worked long hours and often came home streaked with paint and oil, driving a rusting old heap tied together with string. My mum rushed around like a whirlwind, minus the apron, and cake-making was not her strong point. My little brother was rarely tidy or polite, although he did smile a lot. When we finally got a dog it turned out to be slightly nuts, and our cat was a psychopath.

The truth is, families come in all shapes and sizes.

They might not always include a mum, dad, brother, sister and cuddly pet dog . . . perhaps it's just you and your dad, like in *Dizzy*, or maybe you're in a foster family like Paul from *Driftwood*. Perhaps you live with your mum and grandparents, like Jude in *Sundae Girl*, or find yourself coping with a new stepmum and stepsister, like *Scarlett*.

Families are never perfect. They are stressy, strict, embarrassing, infuriating. They make your life more complicated than ever. Sometimes, they drive you crazy, but still, they are your family, and you love them, most of the time at least. It makes sense to learn to live with them.

So . . . can families be trained?

Super Strict? ❀❀❀❀❀❀❀❀

Help, Cathy
My parents are so old-fashioned!
They don't approve of sleepovers,
short skirts, teen mags, make-up . . .
even sweets! And I don't think I'll
be allowed a boyfriend until I'm about
thirty. Help!
      Rhona, age 12

Dear Cathy
My mum and stepdad are super strict. They

set rules that are really hard to keep, and if I miss the bus home on a Saturday, for example, or come in late from a friend's house, I get grounded. I spend so much time grounded it's a miracle I ever set foot outside at all.

Caoimhe, age 11

Rhona and Caoimhe both have strict families, but at least they know the rules, even if they don't agree with them! The question is, can those rules be changed? Well, maybe, with a little gentle persuasion!

Rhona needs to look for a compromise. Perhaps she is happy to put up with the sweet, make-up and teen mag ban in exchange for a girly sleepover with her friends? If so, she can prepare her parents by inviting her friends over and letting them get to know each other, then asking if a small sleepover with just one or two friends is possible – perhaps as a birthday treat? If permission is given, she needs to make sure they have as much fun as possible, but keep inside the rules – no eating chocolate cake in bed at three in the morning while watching horror movies, OK?

If this goes well, Rhona's parents may then allow her to stay over at her friend's houses. By taking things slowly, trying to understand their concerns and sticking to the rules, Rhona can push the boundaries a little.

Full-on make-up may be out, but how about lip gloss/salve on cold days or cover-stick on zitty days? Rhona might try bargaining for a choc bar once a week, on the grounds it's better for your teeth than boiled/jelly sweets. If teen mags are out, she could get together with friends and create her own – like Ginger and Shannon in *GingerSnaps*. Short skirts may be a no-no, but how about jeans? As for boys, the trick is for Rhona to find someone her parents can't help but approve of . . . worth a try, anyway! Keep the lines of communication open and see what you can negotiate.

Caoimhe's problem is slightly different. She knows the rules, but she keeps on breaking them because she doesn't think they're fair . . . and so she keeps on being punished. Caoimhe needs to earn her parents' trust, and that could take forever unless she learns to cooperate. If Caoimhe's parents want her home on a certain bus, there's a reason for it – and every time she fails to appear on time, she shows them that she doesn't care about their rules or their worries. Equally, constantly missing your curfew is a bad plan. If you can't be trusted to be in by nine, why would anyone offer you an extra hour's freedom?

Caoihme needs to accept that if she breaks a rule, she will be grounded . . . logical conclusion? Don't break the rules! If she earns her parents' trust she will find the rules ease up and she is given more freedom because her parents will start to trust her to be where she says she is and get home when she is expected. It's give and take . . . you can't expect to be treated like a young adult if you go on acting like a child!

Hi Cathy
My best friend often lies to her mum about where she is going, who she's with and what she's doing. She says her mum is too strict, but I feel awkward knowing what she's up to and hate it when she uses me as an excuse.

Erica, age 13

Cathy
My parents say I am too young to have a boyfriend, but my crush has asked me out and I so badly want to say yes. It's so unfair . . . nobody else has parents like this.

I am thinking of just not telling them and going out with him anyway.

Gia, age 14

Going behind your parents' back is something I would never advise. Once you start to lie to them, the whole relationship crumbles and there is little respect or honesty left to keep you afloat.

When you are in your parents' care, they need to know where you are, who you are with and how you can be contacted. These are the basics of trust and safety. If something went wrong and your parents didn't know where you were, how could they help? Would Erica's friend be brave enough to call her parents if she got into trouble at a party when they thought she was at a friend's house? Maybe not. You need to be able to ask for help because no matter how sussed you think you are, sometimes things WILL go wrong.

If parents find they are being lied to, then trust me, that is likely to upset and annoy them more than almost anything else. Be honest. If you feel things are unfair, get talking . . . show them they can trust you, help them to take little steps towards giving you more freedom until you achieve the thing you want. Work *with* them, not against them.

Jia may not be able to convince her parents she is ready for a relationship, but she can talk honestly to her crush and explain the situation. She may not be able to see him as a boyfriend, but she can see him as a friend . . . and hope that her parents relax enough to change their views.

Brothers and Sisters

Hello, Cathy
My brother is so spoilt. He is definitely the favourite. He gets away with murder, and my mum gives him everything and I barely get anything!

Seema, age 10

Cathy
My little sister drives me mad. She follows me everywhere, takes my things, tries to read my diary and even listens outside the door when my friends are over. I could strangle her!

Cody, age 13

Dear Cathy

My big sister is going through a really rebellious phase. She's in loads of trouble at school and things aren't much better at home. It's like she hates everyone. I just want my sister back!

Kaitlyn, age 11

Brothers and sisters . . . who'd have 'em? Well, they can be pretty cool, but they can also drive you nuts, I admit!

It's hard when you feel your parents have favourites . . . but ask different kids in a family who the favourites are, and they'd all have different opinions! If you feel things aren't fair, it's worth talking quietly to your parents to let them know you're feeling left out. They may not be able to change things overnight, but perhaps they'll be able to explain why they act the way they do. Try to see their point of view and make an effort to meet them halfway . . . and don't let envy spoil your relationship with a brother/sister. Seema should talk quietly to her parents and clear the air. It may make for a happier atmosphere all round!

Cody's little sister may be annoying, but all she

really wants is attention! She looks up to Cody and is trying to be more like her. If Cody takes time out to make a fuss of her sister sometimes, she'll probably get a whole lot more peace! She could give her little sister a makeover, pass on some unwanted clothes/make-up/music and talk to her about the whole growing-up process. Treating her little sister as a person rather than an irritating little pest will make all the difference.

Kaitlyn's sister is lashing out, perhaps over things that have nothing to do with her family. Kaitlyn is obviously missing the good relationship they once shared. She could try writing a letter to her sister to explain this, or just find a quiet time to talk and remind her sister how much she loves and admires her, no matter what.

This may help, but it could be years before Kaitlyn's sister is ready to let her family get close again. There are no guarantees, but telling someone you love them is never a waste of time . . . try it and see.

Problem Parents . . .

Dear Cathy
My dad's job is under threat and he is so

stressy these days it's a nightmare being anywhere near him. He yells a lot and he's so unfair!

Sara, age 10

Stress can pull a family apart if you let it. Sara's dad is struggling to keep his job and worrying about his family so much he can't quite keep things together when he's actually with them. He may feel he's working as hard as he can, yet nobody really understands. The best thing Sara can do is let the stressy bits wash over her and give her dad a hug when she thinks he might need it – sometimes, actions speak louder than words. Sara should also speak to her mum to get some reassurance. The family have hit a rocky patch, but they can get through it.

Cathy, I really hope you can help . . . My mum is so embarrassing. It's like she wants to be my friend. She dresses much too young and even flirts with my boy-mates, which makes me feel sick. My friends think she's cool, but I can't stand it!

Elin, age 13

Hey
If you think Jude's dad in
Sundae Girl is embarrassing, you
should meet mine. He thinks it's
really funny to wind me up in
front of my mates and he has
a habit of bursting into song in
public. He has a song for every
occasion, and he's not even in tune
half the time. I wish he would
stop!
  Carolyn, age 11

Embarrassing parents . . . well, I hate to break it to you, but they are a fact of life. Most of us will be embarrassed by our parents at some point, and some of us suffer more than most! You can't even get your revenge until much later in life when you have kids of your own . . . and then, of course, the whole cycle continues!

Elin's mum is trying a little too hard to be her daughter's friend . . . but Elin already has friends. She wants a mum! Elin's friends like her mum, so the chances are she's not too cringe-making, but perhaps a gentle heart-to-heart would help the two get along a little better. Elin has to accept that her mum is a bubbly, young-at-heart personality, though . . . and learn to live with it!

Carolyn's dad is unlikely to change. He probably thinks he's funny – well, he might be, to everyone but Carolyn! Instead of seeing your parents as a liability, see them as eccentric, unique, interesting. Laugh with them, don't waste time blushing and wishing you could disappear into a crack in the floor every time they show you up. You are not responsible for them. Smile . . . it's not so bad!

. . . and Parent Problems!

Cathy

Lately, my parents have been fighting a lot and sometimes I get stuck in the middle of it all. Mum has been giving my dad threats about getting divorced. Some nights I cry myself to sleep.

Anniela, age 13

Dear Cathy

In your books the child's parents are either happy or divorced. My parents fight quite a lot - sometimes, my dad leaves the house and I get really scared. He always comes back and says sorry, but I worry that one day they'll split up. I don't think I could cope with that.   Laura, age 11

I feel for Anniela and Laura because my parents argued a lot when I was growing up too. I worried about this and often found myself in the middle of their rows, trying and failing to keep the peace. It really upset me and scared me too.

You know what? They never did break up. They weathered their storms, and stuck together to the end, and I realized that a happy marriage doesn't have to be one with no rows. Arguments can be a way to sort out problems, or at least a way to battle through difficult patches.

Anniela needs to step back from the rows, though, as being caught in the middle is no joke. One parent will use you to get at the other, or just enlist your help in the feud. Sometimes, you might wade in yourself to try to sort things out, but either way it's not a great idea.

This isn't your fight – getting involved will just upset you more, especially if you cannot sort things out for them. And sadly, you can't. It's not easy, but if your parents are arguing a lot, take a deep breath, back off and give them the space to work things out.

Laura is doing something else I once did lots of – worrying about what might happen, and thinking the worst. For me, the worst didn't happen, so all that worry didn't do a thing except keep me awake at night.

But what if the worst had happened? If my parents had split, would it have been the end of the world? If two people cannot solve their problems or find a way to be happy together, if their lives are filled with regret, bitterness, anger or hurt, then is staying together still the best thing? Maybe not.

Laura's parents have a stormy relationship, but they are a long way from breaking up. Laura should let them know how she's feeling – perhaps they can keep some of the rows behind closed doors.

Dear Cathy
My friend's parents are getting divorced
and she's really upset – I don't know

how to cheer her up. Her parents have always seemed OK to me. Can you write a new book similar to that to help me – and my friend?

Maya, age 12

Cathy

My dad has just left us. Nothing makes sense any more – Mum won't stop yelling, my sister won't stop crying and I just can't believe he's gone. He might not love Mum any more, but what about us?

Chrissie, age 12

A family split is hard, especially on the children, but sometimes, sadly, it is the only way forward.

Maya will need to be there for her friend in the weeks and months ahead. She can help by keeping things as normal as possible, but show her support by offering a shoulder to cry on whenever it is needed.

Chrissie is still struggling to accept what has happened. It's important to remember that parents break up because they no longer love each other – they still love YOU. You are not to blame in any way for the split, and although things may feel traumatic right now, they will adjust and settle. You are still a family – just a family who no longer live together all of the time.

Patchwork families

Hey Cathy
I loved your book *Sundae Girl* because I am a bit like Jude – I live with my grandparents and my dad. My mum works abroad so I only see her every few months. Some of my friends think this is a bit weird, but I'm used to things this way.
        Karima, age 11

Hi Cathy
My parents broke up when I was little and I live with my mum, my stepdad, my half-sister and my two stepbrothers. My dad lives in the next town with his girlfriend and new baby. I quite like having a big, complicated family.

I recently read your book Scarlett and I like the idea of a jigsaw family, or one that fits together like the pieces in a patchwork quilt. I love my family, so who cares if they're not exactly like everyone else's?

Clare, age 13

It's no news to Karima and Clare, but families are very rarely like the pictures in the reading books I read way back when I started school. They are not perfect. They come in all shapes and sizes. They may be single-parent, or stepfamilies, or include grandparents, aunts and uncles. They may not be related to you at all. It doesn't matter – they are still families, the people who love you, the people who care, *your* people.

There are all kinds of ways of being a family. The version you have may not be the version you want, but as long as you have love, you'll be OK.

Helpbox

Read It . . .

* *Bringing Up Your Parents* by John Farman
  (Piccadilly)
* *Is Anyone's Family as Mad as Mine?*
  by Kathryn Lamb (Piccadilly)
* *Wise Guides: Divorce and Separation*
  by Matthew Whyman (Hodder)

Websites:

www.kidshealth.org – sections on divorce,
stepfamilies, adoption, fostering and
getting on with your family
www.childline.org.uk – sections on families,
stepfamilies and family relationships
www.itsnotyourfault.org – help and support
for children/teens when a family breaks up

Helplines:

ChildLine – 0800 1111

Stepfamily Scotland – 0845 122 8655

Cathy's Books ... Published by Puffin

* *Shine On, Daizy Star* – when your dad plans an adventure that threatens to pull your family apart . . .
* *Dizzy* – living with a single dad, getting to know mum again after several years . . .
* *Indigo Blue* – coping when a parent is in an abusive relationship
* *Driftwood* – fostering and adoption
* *Scarlett* – coping after a family split, stepfamilies
* *Sundae Girl* – when a parent has problems, living with grandparents, embarrassing families!
* *Lucky Star* – living with a single mum
* *Angel Cake* – family under stress

10. Sad Stuff

I wish I could tell you that life will be kind to you. I wish I could protect you from the bad stuff, the sad stuff, but I can't.

I want you to get out there and live life to the full, making the most of every day, every moment, but that means taking a risk because life is never perfect. You can make it happy, follow your dreams, work hard, have great friends, fall in love and have the best family in the world, but still there are times when life will throw something really tough at you.

Like it or not, it's going to happen, and when it does it will hurt you, scare you, shock you, make you sad or angry or numb, but you will get through – I promise. And how you handle the hard times can make all the difference . . .

Bereavement

Cathy
My grandad was the best ever. He believed in me and understood me and he was teaching me Italian because

☆ 182 ☆

that's where he was born. He was in the hospital for weeks and then he died, and I don't think I will ever get over it. Why does it hurt so much?

Larisa, age 13

Dear Cathy
A terrible thing has happened. My cousin was in a motorbike accident last week and died. He was only eighteen. It's just so wrong that someone so young can die so suddenly. I can't stop thinking about it.

Alana, age 11

The death of a loved one can take the floor out from under your feet. Whether a death follows a long illness or comes right out of the blue, it is always hard to handle.

Larisa was very close to her grandad, and accepting that he is no longer around will take time. Larisa shouldn't keep her feelings to herself – talking about the person who has died can be sad, but will also help her to come to terms with the loss. Talking to family is a good way to find support, but remember that some of your friends will have been through this too – don't shut them out if they offer a shoulder to cry on.

In time, Larisa will find that she can focus on the happy times she shared with her grandad and be glad that she got to know him so well. Some people make a big impression on our lives, and those people help to shape us – they become a part of who we are.

Death doesn't just come for those who have lived a long and happy life, though, as Alana has discovered. Sometimes, it takes people who have barely had a chance to start living, who still had so much more to give, to do. That can be especially hard to accept.

Alana may find her confidence in the world around her is badly shaken – nothing seems safe or sure any longer. We never know what life has in store for us, but that doesn't mean we should live in fear, wrapping ourselves up in cotton wool in case something should go wrong.

It sounds crazy, but maybe we should live every day as if it could be our last. That means packing in as much fun, love, friendship and happiness as we can . . . living life to the full.

If today was your last day on earth, what would you do differently?

* Smile at your crush?
* Do something cool with your friends?
* Cuddle your dog/cat?
* Eat a slice of chocolate cake?
* Thank the school cook for making the best pizza ever?
* Wash up for your mum?
* Revise for a French test so you can say you finally got twenty out of twenty for something?
* Hug your pesky little sister?
* Take two minutes out to be friendly to the quiet kid at school who doesn't seem to have many mates?

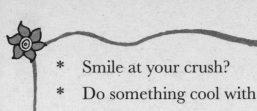

Be your best self, every single day. Life is a gift – make the most of every minute.

Losing someone close to you hurts, big time, but Larisa and Alana will find that time does ease the pain a little. The people we love are always with us . . . never regret the time you had together, even if it was short.

Dear Cathy

The old lady next door has just died, and I am expected to go to the funeral. I'm terrified. I just won't be able to look at the coffin without falling to bits. How can I get through this?

      Harbinder, age 10

Dear Cathy

My auntie died suddenly and we are all going to the funeral. I am dreading it. We will have to wear black and sing sad hymns and that's just not what my auntie was about — she was cool and fun and full of life. It just seems so fake!

      Nita, age 13

Funerals are tough. In the past, children were not always expected to go to funerals in case they were upset, and I didn't go to the funerals of my two grans because I was considered too young. The funny thing is, I really regret not going because I didn't have a chance to say goodbye properly to my lovely grans . . . and saying goodbye is what this is all about.

Going to a funeral is not easy, as Harbinder and Nita are aware. Often, it's a solemn occasion, with flowers and readings and sad hymns, but you won't be the only one who finds it sad. It's OK to let your feelings show, it's OK to cry . . . or not. There are no rules when it comes to how you feel, or how much of your feelings you can show in public.

If you have to go to a funeral, go with family or friends who can support you through it. Yes, it will be sad, but you will find out things about your loved-one's life that can inspire or surprise you too. A funeral doesn't have to be just a sad occasion – it can be a celebration of the person's life as well.

Funerals can be very formal, but not always . . . Nita should check with her family whether wearing black is expected. I have been to funerals where the young people wore every colour of the rainbow, where the coffin was painted with bright patterns, where jokes were told at the altar, where an Abba song was played that made the congregation laugh even as they were crying. And of course, in my book *Sundae Girl*, the family arrive at the church in a pink Cadillac and an ice-cream van, and the family dog is a guest of honour. Why not? A funeral is about celebrating life, as well as mourning death.

Some funerals are very traditional, of course, so it's best to check with family before bending the rules . . . this is not a time to upset or offend anyone if you can help it. If Nita's auntie's funeral is very traditional, she can create her own special way of saying goodbye afterwards.

Once, I was unable to go to the funeral of a very special cousin. I bought white roses and wrote a letter to her, telling her how much she meant to me. Then I walked down across the fields to the river, where I sat quietly and thought about the happy times we had shared. I tore the letter into little pieces and threw it into the river, and threw the roses in one by one and watched as the current carried them away.

Nita might choose a different way to say goodbye, but if it means something to her, it will be the right way.

Funerals are not as scary as you think they will be, but if you truly don't want to go, then don't. Do make sure you find your own way to say goodbye to the person you loved, though . . . it helps, I promise.

When Someone is Ill 🌼 🌼 🌼 🌼 🌼

Dear Cathy
My dad has just had a mini heart

attack and has been told he needs
a bypass operation. I'm so scared
because my granddad died of a
heart attack and now it feels like it's
happening all over again.
                    Jodie, age 11

Cathy
My mum has just been diagnosed
with cancer. I am so frightened
I can't think about anything
else . . . why is this happening
to us?
          Lizbeth, age 12

It can feel very scary and shocking when someone
in your family is seriously ill. Jodie is understandably
worried about her dad, and knowing that her
grandad died of heart disease doesn't help. In fact,
Jodie's dad's mini heart attack is an early warning
signal that he needs to look after his health. By
having the heart bypass operation and making
changes to the way he eats and exercises, he may
find there is a very positive future ahead.

When something goes wrong, it doesn't have to be a disaster – for Jodie's dad, it may be a chance to change while there is still time. Jodie and her family have all had a shock, but knowing there is a problem means you can work with it and do everything possible to live a long and healthy life.

Lizbeth's letter takes me right back to when I was twelve. My mum too had cancer, and I remember the fear and anxiety this created for all of us. Even the word alone is frightening. It's easy to imagine the worst, but most illnesses can be treated. My mum was ill for a long time, but she beat her cancer and those years now seem like a dark and distant memory.

For Lizbeth, finding the facts about her mum's illness will help her to face the tough times ahead. Talking about what is happening and working on simple, practical ways to help each other through will also enable Lizbeth to cope. Neither Lizbeth nor Jodie are alone. They should speak out and let their teachers know what is going on at home so they get the support and backup they need at school, and make sure that their friends are aware of how stressy things are for them right now.

When the going gets tough, it's OK to ask for help.

Hello, Cathy . . .

My mum has MS, so there are a lot of things she can't do. My dad left so it's just the two of us. I have to help out a lot more than any of my friends do. I don't mind that, but it does get tiring and I don't have much time for homework. I don't have much time for a social life, either, and that sucks.

Cazz, age 13

Cathy

My mum has depression and can't look after me or my sisters very well. I am quite good at cooking the tea and getting the shopping, but not so good at making sure everyone has clean clothes for school. Mum says I can't tell anyone in case social services take us into care.

Zara, age 11

Cazz has a lot of responsibility for a thirteen-year-old. She is a 'young carer' and looks after her mum as well as running the house . . . this means that her school work and social life are bound to suffer. If you are looking after a relative, you will need some help and support to do it – everyone deserves a break sometimes.

Cazz needs to make sure her school know how things are at home, so they can help her to keep up with her studies. She also needs to build in time for friends and fun . . . not easy, but those things will really help her to cope the rest of the time. Cazz can contact the Young Carers Association for more support and backup – details are in the Helpbox at the end of this chapter.

Zara's situation is tougher still. She is very young to be looking after her mum and little sisters, and keeping the problem secret just adds to the pressure and stress. Hiding the truth when things go wrong is rarely the right solution.

There is a chance that social services may become involved if Zara tells an adult what is going on, but they would do this to help, not to break up the family. They could make sure Zara's mum had the right medication to feel better, find a friend or relative to offer some extra support and ensure Zara and her sisters are coping. Sometimes, having backup from the social services can be a good thing.

Zara cannot be expected to manage all of this alone

. . . and she shouldn't feel guilty for speaking out and telling a teacher or family friend what's happening. Sometimes, speaking out is the only way.

Scary Stuff

Cathy
I am sometimes bad and when I am, my mum hits me. Sometimes, it leaves bruises and once my teacher asked me what happened, but I said I fell off the swing at home. I know Mum doesn't mean to hurt me, but she does.

Bethany, age 10

Cathy . . .
There is something I wanted to tell you because I think you will understand and maybe be able to tell me what to do. My dad drinks a lot and sometimes it causes big fights and he hits my mum. The worst time was

last Christmas, when he broke her arm.
Nobody knows – everyone thinks Dad
is really nice, but I hate him for what
he does.

Isobel, age 12

Domestic violence is wrong. It's not OK to hit
people . . . end of story.

Bethany knows that what her mum is doing is not
right, and that's why she invented the story about
falling off the swing when her teacher asked about
the bruises. Sadly, though, Bethany believes that
her mum lashes out because she, Bethany, is 'bad'.
If someone tells you you're bad often enough, you
start to believe it – it chips away at your confidence
until you feel worthless.

Bethany isn't 'bad'. Even if she were badly
behaved sometimes, it wouldn't matter – her mum
does not have the right to hit her. Domestic violence
is not the fault of the person being hit. It's all
about the anger and violence bubbling up inside
the one who does the hitting. They are to blame,
always.

Bethany cannot help her mum to get the
assistance she needs to control her temper unless
she speaks out. It will take courage, but she should

talk to the teacher who asked her about the bruises and explain what is going on. Social services may become involved because they will want to be sure that Bethany is not in danger, but once the problem is out in the open both Bethany and her mum can find the help and support they need to build a stronger, more loving relationship – one without violence.

Isobel too is living a lie. Her family looks happy from the outside, but on the inside it's a very different story. Alcohol and violence is ripping the family apart from within, and turning love to hate.

Isobel's first step should be to talk to her mum and ask how she is coping. Talking may help both Isobel and her mum, perhaps paving the way towards finding help and support, or working out how to change things. It may be that Isobel's mum is not ready to face the truth or find the courage to do anything about it. That will be hard, but Isobel can find support elsewhere – a trusted teacher or a helpline can offer help and advice to make her feel less alone.

Living with violence is frightening, so don't try to bottle up the fear. It's OK to speak out and ask for help – you are not alone.

Dear Cathy

Something very bad has happened. Last week, my dad's friend gave me a lift home, and at one point he pulled over and touched me in a really horrible way. He said that I was a little flirt and that I can't tell because nobody would ever believe me. What can I do?

Danielle, age 12

Sometimes, adults let us down badly. Danielle knows that what her dad's friend did was very wrong, but she is scared to speak out. Her abuser has planted a seed of doubt in her mind that she somehow encouraged his behaviour and is somehow to blame.

Danielle is NOT to blame. She didn't flirt, but even if she had it would make no difference . . . her dad's friend is in the wrong. He is an adult, and not only did he betray Danielle's trust and that of her family, he also broke the law. That's why he is so keen for her to stay silent about what happened. What happened to Danielle is sexual abuse, and it is never, ever acceptable.

Danielle must tell her parents what happened.

It won't be easy, but perhaps writing down exactly what happened will make it clearer. Hopefully, Danielle's parents will believe her, although they will be shocked to discover what their 'friend' has done. They may report his behaviour to the police, to stop him from doing the same thing to other young girls, and will almost certainly ensure that he stays away from the house and the family in future.

Occasionally, adults have a hard time believing that things like this can happen. This can leave a young victim feeling very lost, alone and vulnerable. If this happens to Danielle, she should try to understand that her parents are struggling with feelings of guilt, fear and disbelief. Sometimes, it is easier to blank out something scary rather than accept that it happened and deal with the fallout, but in time the truth will sink in. Meanwhile, Danielle can find support by calling ChildLine on 0800 1111 – they will listen, and they really can help.

Nobody, not even a trusted adult, has the right to make you do anything you are not happy to do, or to touch you in ways that make you feel uncomfortable, guilty or bad. Sometimes, the adult may be someone you know well and love, or even, rarely, someone in your own family, and that is very tough. Remember that these things are wrong and find the courage to speak out and get some help and support. If you are not believed right away, go on speaking out until someone listens and helps you.

Sexual abuse wrecks lives. If an abuser goes unreported, he may go on targeting young people and many more lives will be damaged. Don't stay silent . . . help is out there, I promise.

Broken Families

Please help, Cathy
My mum and dad have just split up. My dad was having an affair and my mum is so angry she won't let us speak about him or see him. It's like she wants to wipe him out of our lives. I know what he did was awful, but he's still my dad and I miss him.

        Connie, age 13

Cathy
My dad left a few years ago and has never been good at staying in touch. Now he is going to live in the US and I might never see him again. Mum says

'Good riddance'. I do love my mum, but is it so wrong to want a dad as well?

Joelle, age 11

Divorce and separation doesn't have to be the end of the world, but it can feel that way. And sometimes, if the split is messy, the hurt can go on long after the marriage is over.

Connie is in a difficult situation. Her mum is still very hurt and angry, and is trying to forget that her ex ever existed. This isn't very fair on Connie, who understandably wants to see her dad.

Sometimes, especially in the aftermath of a split, adults can make mistakes. Connie's dad may have behaved badly, but unless he has done anything to threaten or harm his daughter, she should be allowed to keep in touch with him. Connie needs to talk to her mum and explain how she feels . . . it may take time and patience, but hopefully the lines of communication can be rebuilt.

For Joelle, things are tougher. Her dad's way of dealing with the split has been to cut the ties and move on, seeing his daughter only occasionally. Now that he plans to move abroad, Joelle feels she is losing him completely.

Joelle could write to her dad and let him know how much she needs him and wants to keep in touch. Perhaps a long-distance relationship may be easier for him to maintain, but, sadly, it's also possible that he won't keep in touch. Parent-child relationships are not always easy, especially after a break-up – some parents choose to walk away from their old lives, leaving a trail of pain and mess behind them.

Parents are not perfect . . . and when a parent lets us down, it hurts more than almost anything else. Sometimes, children go on trying to make connections with parents who have hurt them, but often they have no choice but to let go. If a parent cannot give you the love and support you need, you may need to look around for others – teachers, relatives, family friends – who can. They won't replace your parent, but it will help, and sometimes that makes all the difference.

Helpbox

Read It . . .

* *Wise Guides: Divorce and Separation* by Matthew Whyman (Hodder)

* *Healing Your Grieving Heart for Teens:
  100 Practical Ideas* by Alan Wolfelt
  (Companion Press)
* *After Someone Dies* (free leaflet available
  from CRUSE Bereavement Care, PO
  Box 800, Richmond, Surrey TW9 1RG
  or download as a PDF file from
  www.rd4u.org.uk)

Websites:

www.kidshealth.org – sections on bereavement,
abuse, and much more

www.childline.org.uk – sections on neglect,
abuse, domestic violence, what happens when
someone dies and more

www.youngcarers.net – help, support and advice
for those caring for a parent/family member

www.rd4u.org.uk – for anyone grieving after the
death of a loved one

www.samaritans.org – when you don't know
where to turn

www.riprap.org.uk – help and support for young
people with a parent who has cancer

www.al-anonuk.org.uk/alateen – help for teenage
relatives and friends of alcoholics

Helplines:

ChildLine – 0800 1111

RD4U Helpline – 0808 808 1677 (for when someone you love has died)

Email:

info@rd4u.org.uk – to ask a question linked to the death of a loved one

jo@samaritans.org – when you don't know where to turn

Write to:

Samaritans: Chris, PO Box 9090, Stirling, FK8 2SA – when you don't know where to turn

Cathy's Books ... Published by Puffin

* *Dizzy* – abandoned by mother
* *Indigo Blue* – domestic violence
* *Driftwood* – living in care, coping with the death of a parent
* *Scarlett* – messy divorce and its aftermath
* *Sundae Girl* – alcoholism, the death of a grandparent
* *Lucky Star* – life on a rough estate, how drugs wreck lives
* *Angel Cake* – money troubles

11. Things That Don't Help ...

So what do you do when things go pear-shaped? Different people react in different ways, but the temptation to lash out and rebel can be strong. Maybe you're feeling angry, hurt, lost or alone, but tread carefully – the way you handle those feelings can shape your future for good or bad.

Let's make sure it's for good!

Don't Worry!

Hi Cathy

I'm so worried that something bad will happen to me or my family. I look around and see all the bad things that go on in the world - terrorism, war, knife crime, even fires and floods. It's got so bad I can't sleep at night. Will this fear go on forever?

Manisha, age 11

Cathy

I'm worried sick about school. My parents expect me to do really well — my sister is studying to be a doctor — but I find some subjects a real struggle. I don't want to let my parents down, but at exam time I'm literally sick with fear.

Gabi, age 14

Some things are going to happen whether you worry about them or not. It makes sense to stay out of danger, avoid war zones, listen to severe weather warnings and take care of your health, but still, some things you cannot predict. Scary, huh? Perhaps we should all hole up in our homes and never venture out again . . . but maybe the floods/ fires/terrorism or earthquakes would come to us. Nowhere is safe. Better just give up then, and be scared and frightened the whole time.

Does worrying help? Not really. Bad things, like those mentioned above, happen very, very rarely. Yes, it's just about possible you may meet a mad axe-murderer on your way to the corner shop, but you're more likely to meet a friend, a neighbour, a cute boy, a bunch of kids, a couple

of rag-taggle dogs. Still going to stay at home worrying?

Better to get out there and enjoy life, every minute of it.

Worry is bad for you. It can make you ill, and it can definitely make you unhappy and take the joy out of life. You can choose whether to allow irrational worry into your life. If, like Manisha, you know your worrying has got out of hand, make a real effort to see all the good things life has to offer and to counter each worry with a more positive thought.

If you're all tied up in knots because your dad's late home from work, don't panic and tell yourself he's been involved in a car crash. It's way more likely there's a traffic jam in town, a last-minute meeting at work or that he's stopped off at the library/pizza takeaway on the way home. Worry is just a voice inside your head, telling you to think the worst . . . and thinking the worst makes you feel bad. Answer that voice back with more sensible, realistic, positive thoughts.

If your worry keeps you awake at night and cannot be chased away that easily, see your doctor and explain how you're feeling. Anxiety can be a medical problem, and there are solutions . . . don't suffer in silence. Sharing your concerns can help put them in perspective, and help you to feel less alone with your problems.

Gabi's worries about school and about letting her parents down can be sorted. Lots of us worry about tests and exams, but wouldn't it be better to revise properly and know we're as ready as we can be for them? That cuts worry to a minimum, as we know we'll be able to do our best – and that's all we CAN do. Gabi is afraid that her best isn't good enough, and that her parents expect more from her than she can give. She needs to talk seriously with them and explain how she feels, perhaps with a teacher's support.

If other people have unrealistic expectations of you, or want something from you that's just not possible for you to give, then that's a problem you need to discuss and sort out as soon as possible. Don't try to be something you're not, or force yourself to jump through hoops in the hope of pleasing others. It's OK to be you.

Little White Lies

Cathy
All the girls in my class have boyfriends and
I invented a boy I'd met on holiday so

they wouldn't feel sorry for me. Now I'm
stuck with pretending he writes to me, and
I don't know how to stop the lie.

Fran, age 12

Dear Cathy
When I moved schools, I told everyone
my parents had really good jobs and that
we had a big house and lots of money. Now
I can't even ask anyone home because
they'll know I was lying . . . I'm in a
real mess.

Lexi, age 10

Little white lies have a way of getting out of hand,
as Fran and Lexi have discovered. Maybe you don't
mean to lie. Perhaps you just want to fit in, impress
your friends, or embellish the truth a little, but pretty
soon you're trapped in a web of secrets and lies.

Lies are easy to tell, and not so easy to put right.
There's only one thing that can wipe out a lie, and
that's the truth. Of course, you can try to wriggle
out of it for a while . . . Fran could always say her
boyfriend has ditched her; Lexi could tell everyone
her family have fallen on hard times. Those aren't
great solutions, though – they just add to the first
lie, make it more tangled and twisted than ever.

The more you lie, the more likely you are to be found out.

People have an instinct for when others are not telling the truth, so the chances are Fran and Lexi's friends already suspect things are not as they seem. You cannot have friendship without trust, and that's why lies can do so much damage. Fran and Lexi must tell the truth, and explain why they lied to start with. Their friends won't be impressed, but they will respect the fact that Fran and Lexi are being honest now. Hopefully, they will forgive them.

Lying won't make others like or accept you – just the opposite. It will add to your troubles . . . and you will be found out. Don't go there.

Self-destruct

Hi Cathy

My parents split up last year and nothing seems to matter any more. I know there is no such thing as a 'happy family'. I can't be bothered with school any more and I've made some new friends who smoke a lot.

I know it's bad for you, but the truth is, I don't really care . . .

Demi, age 13

Demi is hurting. Her life has tilted out of shape and she can't make sense of it any more . . . why work hard at school? Why behave? Why look after your health? The family split has made Demi question everything. She has given up on school, old friends and even on herself, and the person who'll suffer most from this is Demi. She is punishing herself, taking risks with her health and her future.

Smoking damages your health, looks and finances. It's not cool or tough or rebellious, just self-destructive. It's also addictive, so once you're hooked on cigarettes, it takes real effort and determination to break free again . . . but the sooner you stop the sooner you will repair the damage it does.

Thirteen is too soon to give up on the future. OK, things haven't worked out the way Demi expected, but she still has a family – they just don't live together any more. They can still be a happy family, and good friends and a few exam passes could hand Demi back her future too. Demi needs to talk to friends, family, maybe even a school counsellor or guidance teacher about how she's feeling, and find better ways to handle the hurt. Right now, the only person she's punishing is herself.

Cathy

I'm usually really shy, but a few weeks ago I was out at a party and ended up getting tipsy on cider. I was amazed how brave it made me feel. I've done it a few times since, and once I had some wine my parents had left in the house before I went to school. It made me feel like I could cope better, somehow. But it feels a bit scary and out of control too. What should I do?

Tracie, age 13

Dear Cathy

Lately, I've been hanging out with some kids who drink. I've ended up drunk a few times. Once I ended up kissing this boy I'm actually a bit scared of, and a few times I've had really bad hangovers and had to miss school. My mum doesn't even notice or care. I'd like to stop, but I don't know how.

Julianne, age 14

Alcohol is a drug. It can relax you and change the way you feel, as Tracie has discovered. It can also make you do things you might not otherwise do, which is why Julianne found herself kissing a boy she didn't even like. That's not all, though. Alcohol is a poison, and it damages your body and kills off brain cells . . . hangovers are your body's way of warning you off. If it hurts, it's not good!

Tracie is using drink to give herself confidence, but it's a dangerous way to do it. Drink can make you brave, yes, but also foolish. It wrecks your judgement and leads you into bad decisions. And drinking before school is a fast track to disaster . . . Tracie will be found out, and when she is, she'll be in a whole lot of serious trouble. Tracie knows that drink is not the answer. She needs real confidence, the kind that comes from liking, accepting and trusting herself – those things cannot be found inside a bottle.

Julianne also knows that the drinking has to stop. All too quickly, it is leading her into dangerous situations and messing up her school attendance. It sounds as though Julianne wants her mum to notice what's going on – it's almost as though the drinking is a cry for help. Julianne needs to sort things out with her mum – if she feels loved and secure, she won't need to go to such dangerous extremes to get her mum's attention.

Rebel, Rebel ✿ ✿ ✿ ✿ ✿ ✿ ✿ ✿

Dear Cathy
My mum has just remarried, but I don't like my stepdad. He's always trying to tell me what to do, but he's not my dad and he has no right to do that. The more he yells at me to stay in, the more I rebel — I'm thinking of getting my nose pierced because I know that'd drive him mad.

Donna, age 13

Dear Cathy
My parents are so wrapped up in their jobs they barely notice I'm alive. I get nice clothes and presents, but I'd give anything to have strict, loving parents like some of my classmates. Mine let me get away with murder. I've been in loads of trouble at school and they don't even seem to care. Sometimes, I wonder if I'm invisible.

Sienna, age 13

Donna is acting up to challenge her new stepdad. Whatever he says, she'll want to do the opposite – if he suggested burning her school books and dyeing her hair pink, she'd probably settle down and become a straight-A student in perfect uniform. Behaving badly just to spite someone is not a good plan because it allows that person to control you. Surely that's the last thing you want!

Donna's stepdad is doing his best to look out for her safety and wellbeing. He's new at this, so he's bound to make mistakes, but he cares about her and that's why he is making rules and asking her to stick to them. War has been declared here, and the only way forward is to call a truce – Donna's mum may be able to help to calm things down. Until Donna can find a way to get along with her stepdad or tolerate him, at least – she will go on rebelling just to wind him up. And who loses out in the long run? Donna.

Think about it. Getting a piercing is a big decision, and one that should only be made if you're sure it's what you want . . . doing it just to wind someone up is really *not* a good reason!

Sienna is also acting badly to see how far she can push things before her parents notice and give her some attention. The problem is, sometimes, parents are too involved in their own lives to realize what's happening to their kids until it's too late. That's very sad, but the real loser will be Sienna. You only get one shot at life – don't waste that chance. Maybe your family aren't as perfect as they could be, maybe you are hurt or angry or confused . . . but make a mess of your life and you are the loser.

Take control – and start steering your life in the direction you want to go.

Dear Cathy
My friends seem to have so much, but
my mum is out of work and I feel
like the odd one out. Last week I was
looking for a pressie for one of them.
I saw some cool make-up and slipped
it into my bag without paying. Now
I really want to do it again . . . the
shops expect to lose stuff to shoplifters,
so why should I feel bad?
                    Corinne, age 12

Some things are right and some are wrong, full stop.

Stealing – and that's exactly what shoplifting is – is wrong. It doesn't matter that Corinne doesn't have the cash to buy the things she wants – that doesn't give her the right to steal. Would Corinne like it if someone broke into her room and stole her things? No. How about if she built up a successful business, and someone came along and stole the things she'd worked so hard for? I don't think she'd like that either, yet that's just what she's doing to someone else's business every time she steals.

If Corinne shoplifts again, sooner or later, she will be caught. When that happens, she will be prosecuted and her parents will be called in. Corinne could end up with a police caution, or worse, a criminal record.

It's not OK to take things just because you think you deserve them. You need to earn those things – if you do that, they'll mean even more to you. No, it's not fair that some people have more than others, but that's the way things are. If you don't get enough pocket money, find a part-time job or offer to babysit/walk the dog/ weed the garden for family friends and neighbours. If you can't afford fancy pressies, get creative and make something personal and unique.

Looking for Love?

Dear Cathy

I've never been pretty or popular,
and even my mum acts like she's
ashamed of me. Last year, though,
I realized I had a good figure and
boys fancied me. I've had quite a few
boyfriends now, and kids at school
call me horrible names. I suppose I
have a bad reputation, but I just
want to be loved - is that so wrong?

Roisin, age 15

Wanting to be loved is never wrong, but Roisin may be looking for love in the wrong places. It's pretty clear from her email that she wants the love and support of her mum and her classmates, but because that isn't happening, she's settled for a different kind of love. Having lots of boyfriends is not a great way for Roisin to feel valued and cared for . . . after all, she's had lots of relationships in a short time, so no one relationship is lasting for long.

A teenage boy who has lots of girlfriends is often

admired and seen as 'a bit of a lad'. A teenage girl who behaves the same way is often labelled a 'slag'. Not very fair, is it?

Roisin is looking for love, but I'm worried that her boyfriends are looking for something very different. When they find it, they drop Roisin and move on, and she ends up feeling rejected again . . . until the next boy comes along. Roisin has to learn to love herself, to realize that she is special and that her love is too valuable to fritter away on boys who aren't really interested in finding that out. If Roisin can build some self-esteem and treat herself with respect and kindness, she may find better friends and maybe even a boy who will be worth falling for.

Hurting Inside ❀ ❀ ❀ ❀ ❀ ❀ ❀

Dear Cathy

Things are very bad at home. Sometimes, I just can't stand it and I cut myself. It sort of takes away the stress, but only for a while because then I feel really, really disgusted with myself. I can't tell anyone about this.

Mel, age 12

Dear Cathy

What do you do if you can't see the point any more? If you just don't want to get out of bed in the morning or carry on with life? That's how I feel.

Kathryn, age 14

Self-harm is the ultimate way of punishing yourself, of causing yourself some physical pain to match the emotional hurt inside. It doesn't solve any problems, though, as Mel has realized – feeling two kinds of pain isn't exactly an improvement. Self-harm can become a habit that's hard to break, but it's very dangerous and Mel must get some help to stop the impulse.

Yes, it's hard to talk about self-harm. Her friends and family may be shocked and frightened by it, but it's important for Mel to speak out – this is too tough for her to handle alone. Her family and doctor can offer support and counselling to help Mel find better ways to handle the stress that triggers this. Self-harm is hard to hide for long, and no matter what the problems at home, there will be answers.

Kathryn is past the point of looking for answers. She is so low she can't really see a future, and everything seems grey and dull and pointless. If you feel like this for more than the odd day or so, you are probably depressed. Depression is an illness, and help is out there – both medication and counselling that can work together to lift the cloud and help you to find the joy in life again.

Never be afraid to ask your doctor for help with something like this. Things can go wrong with your mind as well as your body. That doesn't mean you're crazy – you're only crazy if you don't ask for the help you need to feel better! Seriously, though, when you're feeling low it can be hard to see a way out of the gloom. If you notice a friend or classmate struggling in this way, don't just turn away – ask them how they are, or tell a trusted teacher that you're concerned.

Think about it . . . no matter how bad you're feeling, this is not the time to give up. When you hit rock bottom, the only way is up!

Food Wars

Dear Cathy
My parents are going through a rough patch. I've got into the habit of snacking on chocolate, sweets and cake when I feel upset. To be honest, it's more than

snacking . . . I can eat a whole pack of biscuits at one sitting and two or three chocolate bars. Then I feel worse than ever because I'm overweight anyway and I know this is making it worse. I just can't help it.

Lottie, age 11

Just as an addiction to cigarettes or drink is bad news, using food to dull down your unhappiness won't help you to feel better. The stress at home is upsetting Lottie, and bingeing on sugary snacks is a way she has evolved to help her cope. Sadly, it just doesn't work – as Lottie says, it just makes things worse. I know how Lottie feels – I have a sweet tooth and a tendency to comfort eat when the going gets tough, but like her, I have learnt that a bar of chocolate (or three) can't solve my problems.

Lottie has to talk to her parents and get some support at school to help her through this difficult time . . . finding better ways to handle the problem that triggers the overeating is the way forward, but of course, she'll have to tackle the binge eating too.

Breaking any addiction is hard. Lottie can make sure she doesn't buy the foods she likes to binge

on, and ask her parents to make sure they don't either. At crunch times, saying, 'Yes, I can eat that chocolate bar, but not for ten minutes,' gives her a breathing space to think about whether she really wants to do it. At the end of ten minutes, she can bargain again, until she begins to regain control – this can work with giving up any addiction, from smoking to self-harm. Lastly, Lottie will find many positive ways to deal with her mixed-up feelings in the next chapter – overeating doesn't help, but there are lots of things that do.

Dear Cathy

I have always been a bit chubby and I hate it. My family are all big and we don't eat the healthiest food, but I've found a way round it by making myself sick after I've eaten. Nobody knows. It sounds a bit yukky, but it won't actually do me any harm, will it?

Sue, age 13

Help!
My friends keep saying I'm too thin and my family are always

trying to make me eat, but I'm not thin at all, I'm fat! I hate that they want me to stay this way. Even the teachers are on my case now because they found out I've been throwing my packed lunch away. How can I get them to leave me alone?
    Stacey, age 12

Often, people with an eating disorder don't even realize they have a problem. Some, like Sue, feel they've discovered a great new way to stay slim . . . but bulimia, or making yourself sick/using laxatives after eating can wreck your health for good. Others, like Stacey, look in the mirror and see rolls of fat where other people see little more than a skeleton . . . anorexia is an illness that messes with your head at the same time as it starves your body.

Eating disorders can kill you, like a slow form of suicide. In less extreme cases, they can damage your internal organs and digestive system, mess up your hormone levels and cause hair loss, tooth decay, excess body hair and skin problems. So to answer Sue's question, yes, bulimia will harm you . . . big style.

The best way to stay slim and fit is to eat healthy foods like protein (meat, fish, egg, dairy, soya, quorn, beans); whole grains (pasta, wholemeal bread, rice and so on); and fresh fruit and vegetables. Some fat is fine – but think olive oil in a salad dressing or a few almonds rather than a family-size pack of crisps or a cream cake. Cut down on junk foods, sweets and fizzy drinks, and take regular exercise every day or two – something like cycling, swimming, running, tennis or aerobics that raises your heart rate a little.

 If you are worried about your weight, see your doctor and ask for advice. Your body is still growing, so dieting is not a good idea, but your doctor may suggest a healthy eating plan. If Sue cannot stop the impulse to make herself sick after eating, though, she must see her doctor and get some specialist help and support to break frcc of the bulimia.

Stacey's email rings real alarm bells. Anorexia has a tight grip of her, and unless she can see what's happening for herself, this battle will be a tough one to win. Stacey's email to me suggests that perhaps one small part of her, at least, knows that things have got way out of control. When she starts to see why those around her are so worried, she may begin to turn things around – with the right medical help and counselling.

If you suspect that a friend is anorexic or bulimic, tell a guidance teacher your concerns – in confidence, if that is easier – and let your friend know that although you're worried, you are always there for her. Be supportive, and let her talk if she needs to. Try not to judge, but don't encourage her eating disorder – and get some support for yourself. Propping up a friend with an eating disorder can be hard work emotionally – make sure you look after yourself too.

And what if you feel yourself sliding towards an eating disorder? Speak out and get some help as soon as you can – before it takes control of you. You cannot fix the problems in your life by being thin, nor by punishing yourself with starvation, bingeing or vomiting. Read through chapters six and seven again and boost your confidence, make friends with the real you . . . and remind yourself that food is not a friend or even an enemy, it's just a fuel.

If you've lost sight of that, find some help and support – today.

Running Away ❀❀❀❀❀❀❀❀

Dear Cathy
I am so unhappy at home I cannot

stand to stay there another minute.
Nobody understands me, or even wants
to. I feel so unloved. I dream of
running away, finding proper friends
and a better life. And then maybe my
parents would be sorry.

Jordann, age 13

Running away to find a better life . . . well, maybe.
The reality of running away is a little less romantic.
Homelessness, begging, drugs, prostitution, hunger,
fear, exploitation . . . young people who run away
from home are easy prey for lowlifes and criminals
who will use them in whatever ways they can.
Runaways are perhaps the most vulnerable of
all young people, and life on the streets is tough,
dangerous and very, very frightening.

Jordann is angry at her family and hurt too. Yes,
running away would make her parents sorry, but
Jordann would be the real loser. Better to stay and
sort her problems, or learn to live with their failings
until she is old enough to find a college/uni course
or job that enables her to move away from home
safely. Runaways run straight into danger . . . it is
never, ever a solution.

All of the girls in this section are upset, angry, hurt or unhappy about something in their lives, but instead of facing their problems and trying to solve them, they have come up with ways to cope that actually bring them more heartache and grief.

You cannot find a solution to your problems by eating chocolate cake, drinking cider or smoking a cigarette. Piercing your nose won't help, and nor will tearing up your maths homework or kissing the boy in Year Ten with hands like an octopus. Hurting yourself, starving yourself, lying, stealing, running away . . . none of those things help. They might distract you, or make you forget for a little while, or help you to hide a little. They might make the pain you're feeling inside a physical thing too. They might punish you by making you feel bad about yourself, or ashamed, or embarrassed.

The only way to fix a problem is to look at it head-on and work on ways to solve it, often with help and support from others. It's not easy, but it's the only way.

That doesn't mean there's nothing you can do to help yourself feel better in the meantime, though . . . because some ways of coping really *do* work. Read on . . .

Helpbox

Read It . . .

* *Worried About Self-Injury?* (YoungMinds booklet with lots of helpful advice and support; contact YoungMinds on 0870 870 1721 or download as PDF file from *www.youngminds.org.uk/publications/all-publications/worried-about-self-injury)*

* *Do You Ever Feel Depressed?* (YoungMinds booklet on how to cope with depression; contact YoungMinds on 0870 870 1721 or download as PDF file from *www.youngminds.org.uk/publications/all-publications/do-you-ever-feel-depressed*)

* *Together We Will Beat Eating Disorders* (leaflet/PDF file from Beat, a UK charity aiming to beat eating disorders; call 01603 753305 or download as PDF file from www.b-eat.co.uk/Publications/Leaflets)

Websites:

www.childline.org.uk – sections on when someone dies, feeling sad, running away, crime, drugs

www.youngminds.org.uk – go to 'My Head Hurts' section for info on depression, self-harm, eating disorders and more

www.samaritans.org – when you don't know where to turn

www.quitbecause.org.uk – helping young people to quit smoking

Helplines:

ChildLine – 0800 1111

Beat Youthline – 0845 634 7650 (Mon–Fri 16.30–20.30, Sat 13.00–16.30)

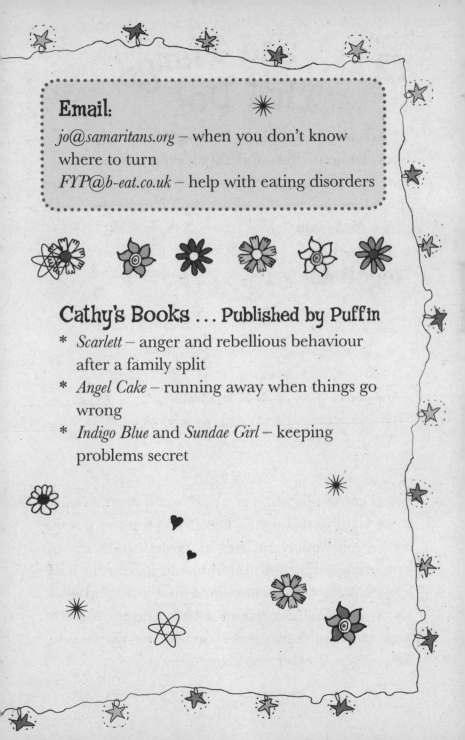

Email:

jo@samaritans.org – when you don't know where to turn

FYP@b-eat.co.uk – help with eating disorders

Cathy's Books ... Published by Puffin

* *Scarlett* – anger and rebellious behaviour after a family split
* *Angel Cake* – running away when things go wrong
* *Indigo Blue* and *Sundae Girl* – keeping problems secret

12. ... and Things That Do!

This chapter is full of ways to help you communicate, relax, let go of hurt and anger, express yourself . . . and find support, help and happiness. Those are the things that really *can* help you handle the tough times. Yes, really!

Negotiate!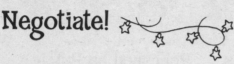

Dear Cathy
I want my parents to see that they can trust me and give me a bit more freedom, but every time I try to discuss it, I get really annoyed and end up storming off.
They can be so unfair.
                               Eloise, age 12

Good communication is a skill we all need to learn if we want to succeed in life! If you want to discuss something important, negotiate new rules or say something important, but difficult, it helps to have a plan. Note down what you want to say and what you want to achieve from the chat, and think about how you can make sure you will be listened to. So . . . how do you negotiate?

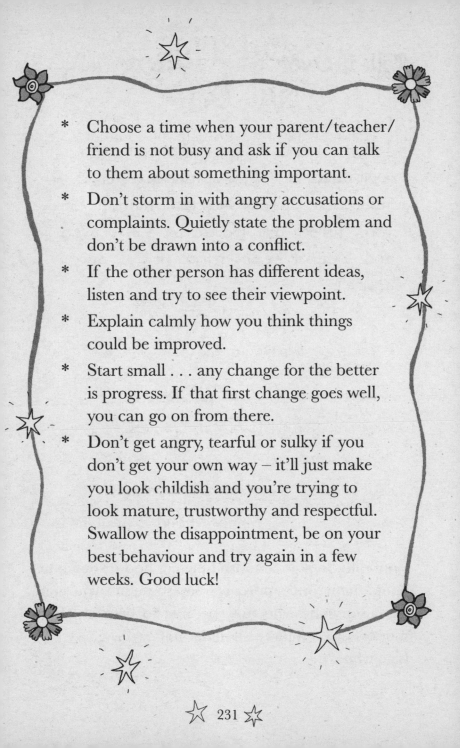

* Choose a time when your parent/teacher/ friend is not busy and ask if you can talk to them about something important.

* Don't storm in with angry accusations or complaints. Quietly state the problem and don't be drawn into a conflict.

* If the other person has different ideas, listen and try to see their viewpoint.

* Explain calmly how you think things could be improved.

* Start small . . . any change for the better is progress. If that first change goes well, you can go on from there.

* Don't get angry, tearful or sulky if you don't get your own way – it'll just make you look childish and you're trying to look mature, trustworthy and respectful. Swallow the disappointment, be on your best behaviour and try again in a few weeks. Good luck!

Talk It Over

Dear Cathy
I don't know if you remember my last email, but I have decided to take your advice and talk to my form tutor. The trouble is, I'm scared and I can't seem to do it . . . any advice?

Leigh, age 11

Dear Cathy
Some very bad stuff has been happening and I know I need to tell someone, but I just don't know who. What if they don't believe me?

Kristina, age 12

Confiding in someone isn't easy. Choose someone sympathetic and approachable, someone you can trust, someone who may be able to help or offer support or even just a shoulder to cry on.
Like who?

* a guidance teacher
* any teacher who seems approachable and sympathetic
* a year head
* a school counsellor
* a school nurse
* your family doctor
* your gran, grandad, aunt, uncle, cousin or other family member
* a neighbour
* a friend
* a friend's mum/dad
* a family friend
* a priest/vicar/rabbi or someone similar
* a social worker
* a mentor
* a youth worker
* a helpline

How do you do it? Wait until they have some free time and ask if you can talk in private. Take a deep breath and tell them what is worrying you, or, if it's too hard to say it out loud, write it down in a letter. You will almost certainly be believed, but if you are not, go on telling and asking for help until you are taken seriously. Once things are out in the open, it won't feel so daunting – and you can begin to talk about what might happen next. Sometimes, enlisting some adult help is the only way forward.

Expert Help

Dear Cathy
I have a very embarrassing problem. I need to see my doctor, but I'd rather see a woman doctor and I really don't want my mum going along! Help!

                Brooke, age 13

Dear Cathy
My doctor wants me to see a therapist to help me unravel some bad stuff that happened last year. I don't want to. I hate that people might think I'm mad or something. Shouldn't I be able to sort it out myself?

                Freya, age 12

Doctors . . . they can seem scary, but they're there to help us. They've seen just about everything, so nothing you say is going to shock or embarrass them. Sometimes, when you have a girly kind of problem, like Brooke, you may prefer to see a woman doctor, and that's OK. You may be registered with a male doctor, but you can still request an appointment with a female doctor within the same practice. If there isn't one, you can ask for a female nurse to be present.

At thirteen, Brooke is probably old enough to see the doctor without her mum in tow, but she should tell her mum if she can. Mums have a lot of life experience and Brooke's will probably be able to set her mind at rest and help her to take the problem in her stride. She'll also understand that sometimes, staying in the waiting room is the best way to be supportive! Brooke should make an appointment, and now – she may be worrying over nothing, but one thing's for sure, the problem won't go away on its own. If you need to see a doctor, do it – before things get any more serious.

Accepting that you need help for a problem that is mental rather than physical can be tough. Like Freya, many young people feel they should be able to deal with the bad things that have happened to them, chase away depression and conquer unhealthy behaviours, compulsions and ideas.

Sadly, it's not that easy . . . struggling to cope with difficult stuff can be tough. Who says you have to cope alone? If you fell into the ocean and someone threw you a lifebelt, would you ignore it on the basis that you *should* be able to save yourself? That would be kind of crazy. If someone offers you a lifeline, reach out and take it . . . it has to be better than drowning, right?

Counselling or therapy can really help with depression, addiction, self-harm, troubled feelings and a whole raft of other problems that can tangle up your head and your heart. Therapy works . . . it helps you to untangle the mess and create new, more positive lines of thought. It helps to deal with difficult stuff from the past and find new pathways to the future.

It doesn't mean you're sad or mad – just the opposite; it shows you have the courage and determination to tackle the problem. If someone offers you a helping hand, take it – drop the mask and stop pretending you can do it all alone. None of us can – we all need help, sometimes.

Feeling Understood

Dear Cathy
I love your books. I swear I'd go
nuts if I couldn't step into the cool
worlds you've created and hang out
with characters like Ginger, Sam,
Scarlett, Kian and Mouse . . . your
books keep me sane!
                              Ally, age 12

Dear Cathy
People give me stick because I love bands
like MCR, YouMeAtSix and Green Day, but
I love them so much — it's like they really
understand ME, somehow. Those songs say
what I'm feeling!
                              Mandy, age 13

Reading and listening to music are two of my
favourite ways to relax when life gets stressy . . .
maybe they'd work for you too? Like Ally, I love to
open the pages of a novel and fall into someone
else's daydream . . . it's a perfect escape. It's a
great feeling when you identify with a character or

situation, or feel that the story has captured your imagination, taught you something or really got you thinking. When I'm really busy, I'll wake up extra early so as not to miss out on that little chunk of fantasy time . . . again, like Ally, it keeps me sane.

For Mandy, listening to music is like that too. The bands she likes make her feel understood, accepted. She learns from the songs, sees her feelings reflected in the lyrics and expressed in the music . . . no wonder kids who like the same bands connect so easily! There are some bands I feel this way about too . . . bands whose lyrics and music seem to have a hotline to my soul.

Whether you're dancing around the living room in your PJs to a happy tune or hugging your pillow and wiping away the tears as a sad song plays, listening to music is cool. Bit by bit, you are putting together the soundtrack of your life!

Express Yourself!

Dear Cathy
Nobody told me being a teenager
would be so stressy. School, tests,
stroppy friends, crazy parents, boys

who can't decide what or who they want . . . I'd go mad if I didn't have my piano playing. I pour all my feelings into playing and it definitely helps me to cope.

Emz, age 13

Hello Cathy!
I love acting. I'm quite shy, but when I'm playing a part I forget myself completely and almost become the character. I love it . . .

Naomi, age 14

Hi Cathy
I love dance. I do ballet, modern and street and I practise every day. If I'm feeling down, dancing always cheers me up – it's just the way I express myself and my feelings.

Maddy, age 12

Some hobbies are creative, expressive and imaginative . . . they can really help us to channel our feelings and energy into something positive and cool. Emz, Naomi and Maddy are lucky they have hobbies that they can really pour themselves into, hobbies that are an escape, a challenge. A hobby that you love can be a lifesaver.

What if you don't have a hobby? Research suggests that learning new things can boost our self-esteem and happiness levels, so maybe it's time to find yourself a great new hobby! Whether it's learning the saxophone (like Sam Taylor in *GingerSnaps*) or learning how to bake cool cakes (like the ones in *Angel Cake*), a new hobby could put a smile on your face for keeps!

Hey
I'd love to be a writer like you when I am older. I am hooked on inventing stories . . . my life is pretty dull and sometimes stressy, but when I'm writing a story I get to be in control for a change!
Pam, age 12

Cathy
I love writing poetry and song lyrics. It's like all my secret, inside feelings pour out on to paper and turn into something new and

amazing. My dad died last year
and seriously, without the poetry,
I don't know how I'd have coped.

Lainey, age 14

Like Pam, I was hooked on writing stories from
early on. And like Pam, my life was far from perfect
back then! I loved the way I could pull the strings in
a story and control what happened, and also how I
could write about exciting, romantic, adventurous
things, even when my real life just wasn't like that!

Like Lainey, I turned to poetry when I wanted
to deal with big emotions like grief, love and loss. I
wrote acres of dreadful poetry as a teenager, but it
helped me through some difficult times! Pam and
Lainey are expressing themselves on paper, dealing
with difficult feelings and polishing their writing
skills too. Pretty cool.

Hiya, Cathy!
I have your *Dreams & Doodles
Daybook*. I have to hide it under the
mattress in case my little brother
finds it, but it's worth it. I love
recording the ups and downs of every

day . . . it helps me to make sense of my life!

Flick, age 12

Dear Cathy
When I am feeling really upset or angry, I write it down, as a letter to the person who upset me. I don't ever send the letter, but it helps me get my anger out without making the row any worse . . . then I feel better and usually I am able to patch things up and move on! My mum gave me this tip, and it really works for me.

Jamila, age 11

Flick and Jamila are also using writing to help them cope with tricky times. Writing in a diary or journal can help you to reflect on what's going on in your life, and work out how to handle things. Writing letters to soak up negative feelings is also a great idea . . . getting the feelings out is often enough to remove the hurt from a situation and help us to decide how to deal with it. Just don't send the letter . . . unless you are ready for a big showdown or heart-to-heart!

Get Moving!

Hey Cathy
I love swimming, I'm in a club and swim most days. When I don't or can't for some reason, I miss it like mad. My friends say I'm addicted, but it keeps me fit, focused and chilled out, so I don't really care!
                                        Tara, age 13

Sport and exercise don't just keep you fit and slim, as Tara has discovered – they soak up stress and boost your mood by releasing feel-good chemicals called endorphins. That's got to be good! Some of us love the challenge of doing something physical, pushing ourselves to be the best we can be, and that kind of focus and challenge is a buzz for Tara too.

Regular exercise is a great way to cope with sad or stressy feelings . . . it's a win-win activity. Find something you like to do – swimming, cycling, running, tennis, netball, footy, aerobics, step, kick-boxing, gymnastics . . . it doesn't matter. Go for it!

Believe It or Not . . . ❀ ❀ ❀ ❀ ❀ ❀

Dear Cathy

My friends know I am from a very religious family, but they don't really get it. I wish they could see how much I get from going to church and having something to believe in that is 'bigger than me', if that makes sense. It makes me feel safe and looked after.

Elizabeth, age 11

Dear Cathy

I got a meditation CD for my birthday and I do a bit every day, and I think I am much calmer because of it! My mum wants me to go to yoga classes with her, so I might give that a try too.

Courtney, age 13

Religion can be a real help when the going gets tough. The same applies whichever religion it is — it's the fact that you believe it, that you worship/pray regularly and are part of a big community of fellow believers that seems to make the difference. If you have questions, doubts, worries, problems, religion can help you to find answers and to feel less alone. Although Elizabeth's friends don't understand, they might just envy the confidence it gives her. Never knock someone because of their beliefs/religion . . . it may not be right for you, but if it works for them, that's what matters.

Meditation is another great tool for coping with everyday stress. It sounds a little crazy, but research has shown that people who meditate really are calmer and healthier because of it, so Courtney is definitely on the right track! Adding yoga to the mix would probably help even more . . . this one's a winner.

Back to Nature

Dear Cathy
When I get all wound up I take the dogs
out (we have two bearded collies) and walk
across the fields near our village for a
while. I love being in the countryside and
it never fails to help me get things
in perspective.   Rhiannon, age 12

Dear Cathy

If I have a bad day, I plan lots of treats like a bubble bath and a manicure and an early night curled up with one of your books. That always puts a smile back on my face!

Miya, age 13

Nature can be a great healer. Like Rhiannon, I love trudging with my dog through woods or beside rivers, lakes and streams . . . or better still, along a deserted beach! Nature is beautiful and my problems always seem smaller and more manageable after a long walk. Try it and see! The dogs will be your friends for life too . . .

Miya has found that a pamper day works well to boost her mood when she's feeling low . . . having little treats to look forward to when life isn't going according to plan really can make all the difference. Be kind to yourself . . . you deserve it!

Good Stuff!

Dear Cathy
When I've had a bad day, nothing cheers me up like being with my best mates. They always know when to distract me, when to listen and when to offer a shoulder to cry on. My best friends really do rock!

     Tamar, age 11

Dear Cathy
Have you heard of free hugs? I think the world needs more hugs, and going up to a friend and giving them a random hug is a great way to brighten up their day.

     Esta, age 13

Friendship is one of the best ever fixer-uppers when you're feeling down. Who knows you better than your friends? Who can make you smile, or hug you when you cry, better than they can? Unlike family, friends don't *have* to be there for you. They're there because they want to be, because they like you, because they care.

An hour spent with a good friend is priceless. Don't shut your friends out if you are feeling sad or have a problem. Bottling up your worries just allows them to grow – be brave and share your feelings. Your friends can help because often they've been there too . . . they really can get you through.

Esta is right, the world needs more hugs. And she's not the only one to think so . . . in 2004, an Australian guy started giving out free hugs in the street, and his campaign was so successful it has spread to the four corners of the earth. If it hasn't spread to your school yet, see if you can do something about that! Hugging a friend for no reason in particular is a great way to make them – and you – feel better. Time to bring the free hugs movement to your town!

Dear Cathy
I have lots of friends, but one of them,
Edie, is an 81-year-old lady who lives just
up the road. She tells me all about what

things were like in the war, and makes me
hot chocolate. In return I walk her dog
and fetch shopping for her when she needs
it. It feels good to help.

Kirby, age 12

Dear Cathy
I loved your book GingerSnaps,
especially Sam's idea of 'random
acts of kindness'. I started doing
one every day and it's been
brilliant . . . the feeling you get
when you help someone else is
great. It makes me a LOT less
moany about my own problems,
somehow!

Sahail, age 13

Helping others is a great way to forget your own
troubles and make a difference to the world.
When you stop being so wrapped up in your own
problems, you get to see the bigger picture – and
often realize that things aren't so bad after all. And
even if they are bad, you'll maybe see that you can
still come through . . .

Helping other people, whether it's one elderly neighbour or a scattering of 'random acts of kindness', gives you the chance to do something good, something kind, caring, lasting. And that will make you feel good about yourself . . . I promise!

Dear Cathy
It sounds a bit weird, but last year, when my mum was ill, I realized how lucky I was to have her at all . . . we came through the illness together, as a family, and we all appreciate each other a lot more now. There is a lot of good stuff in my life — friends; family; my boyfriend, Jake; macaroni cheese; chocolate profiteroles; blue skies; crumpets. Those things were always there — I just notice them more now!

Imara, age 12

Saying thank you for the good stuff . . . well, it's only polite, right? And as Imara has sussed, it really helps to focus on the good stuff. It's logical, really – negative stuff makes you feel negative, positive stuff makes you feel good. Find something to be grateful for every day and you really will boost your moods and beat the blues.

The Fab Five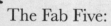

So . . . some things make you feel happy. It's official! These are just a few tips to get you started, but I bet you have lots more ideas that help you to hang on to the feel-good factor! Basically, if you feel low, don't bottle it up. Speak out, get help, and do something positive to help yourself feel better.

Scientists reckon there are five main areas to cover if we want to get happy . . . it's a bit like those five-a-day fruit and veggie servings that help us keep our bodies fighting fit!

The Fab Five:
* doing regular physical activity
* having strong friendships and family ties
* doing things to help others
* being curious, glad and thankful for the world around us
* learning new stuff

Sounds good to me. Grab yourself a helping of happiness and live life to the full . . . starting right now.

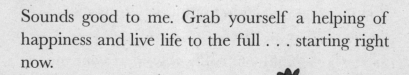

The very last word goes to one of my readers who sent an email so packed with wise words, I couldn't think of anything better to end this chapter . . . and this book.

There is so much more to life than meets the eye. You don't need boys and clothes and loads of A grades and cool hair and money and all that stuff. Really. You don't need it. But you do need love and compassion and empathy and friends and knowledge and a spirit that can't be broken. Life's about living and laughing and loving and helping others and standing up for your beliefs. It's about taking a risk. So jump on board and enjoy the ride . . . who knows where you'll end up?

Y'know what? I couldn't put it better myself.

Lots of love,
Cathy Cassidy xxxx

Helpbox

Check Out:

* activities at your local sports centre
* dance/martial arts classes
* summer schools or evening classes to learn a new skill
* lunchtime clubs/after-school activities
* opportunities for voluntary work
* Girl Guide Groups/Woodcraft Folk – get involved!
* church youth groups/playschemes (to join or to help!)
* the pinboards at your school/library/ community centre
* get together with friends and start your own band/magazine/dance group
* join your local drama group or sign up to learn to ice skate
* stock up with sketchbooks and paints . . . or chop up an old dress and turn it into something new and cool . . .

There are a million cool things to get involved in . . . the only limits are your imagination. What are you waiting for? Get out there and find yourself a life!

Websites:

www.childline.org.uk – sections on feeling sad, helping a friend

www.cathycassidy.com – send in a picture or poem, enter the writing comp, check out the Cathy Cassidy & ChildLine page, find out more about the books . . . and check out the cool, free downloads and ideas to help you celebrate friendship!

Helplines:

ChildLine – 0800 1111

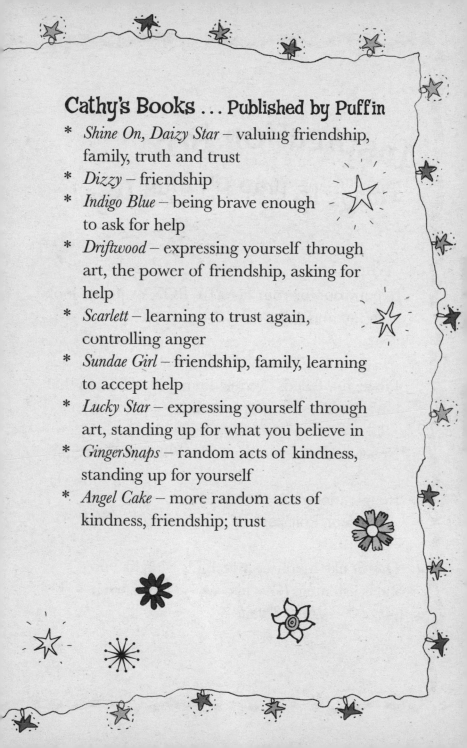

Cathy's Books ... Published by Puffin

* *Shine On, Daizy Star* – valuing friendship, family, truth and trust
* *Dizzy* – friendship
* *Indigo Blue* – being brave enough to ask for help
* *Driftwood* – expressing yourself through art, the power of friendship, asking for help
* *Scarlett* – learning to trust again, controlling anger
* *Sundae Girl* – friendship, family, learning to accept help
* *Lucky Star* – expressing yourself through art, standing up for what you believe in
* *GingerSnaps* – random acts of kindness, standing up for yourself
* *Angel Cake* – more random acts of kindness, friendship; trust

Inspiration Box
Things to Help on Blue Days!

To copy out for your HAPPY BOX or just to look at on sad and rainy days . . .

'I have not failed. I've just found 10,000 ways that don't work!' – **Thomas Edison**

'Never, never, never give up' – **Winston Churchill**

'Imagination rules the world'
– **Napoleon Bonaparte**

'Dance like no one is watching. Sing like no one is listening. Love like you've never been hurt . . .' – **Mark Twain**

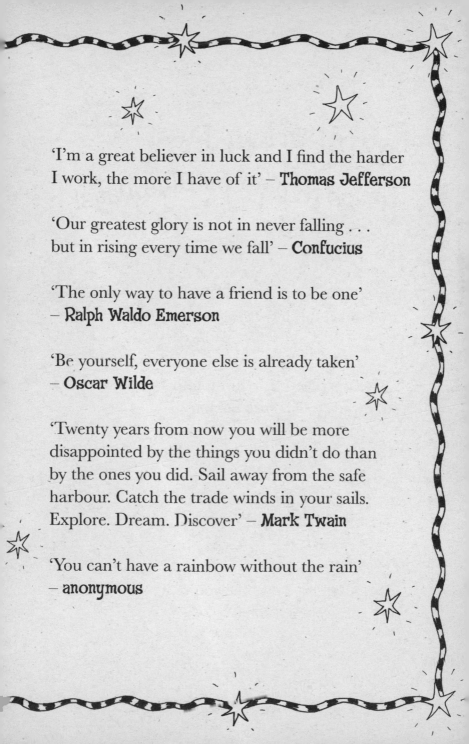

'I'm a great believer in luck and I find the harder I work, the more I have of it' – **Thomas Jefferson**

'Our greatest glory is not in never falling . . . but in rising every time we fall' – **Confucius**

'The only way to have a friend is to be one' – **Ralph Waldo Emerson**

'Be yourself, everyone else is already taken' – **Oscar Wilde**

'Twenty years from now you will be more disappointed by the things you didn't do than by the ones you did. Sail away from the safe harbour. Catch the trade winds in your sails. Explore. Dream. Discover' – **Mark Twain**

'You can't have a rainbow without the rain' – **anonymous**

Random Acts of KINDNESS

Copy cool Sam Taylor from *Gingersnaps* and try a random act of kindness everyday. Here are a few to start you off . . .

- ❤ **WASH UP** without being asked
- ❤ **HUG** a friend!
- ❤ **TALK** to someone who's feeling lonely or left out
- ❤ **COMPLIMENT** a classmate on his/her appearance
- ❤ **SEND A CARD** to your BF for no reason at all
- ❤ **CARRY SHOPPING** for an elderly neighbour
- ❤ **PLAY** with your little bruv/sister – it's fun!
- ❤ **SMILE** – it's free, and it makes everyone feel good. Especially you!

And why not show your BFs how much you care by organizing something that you could do together? The most important thing is spending time with each other and having fun!

❤ **THROW A MINI PARTY FOR YOUR BEST FRIENDS** – you could all watch a DVD together, or make your own dream flags to hang in your room. Or maybe you could bake your own Angel Cakes!

❤ **HOLD A CAKE SALE** – once you've baked your yummy cakes, why not set up a stall to sell them? Maybe you could raise money for a charity that really means something to you.

❤ **INVITE YOUR FRIENDS TO A CLOTHES-SWAPPING PARTY** – you might not be in love with that sparkly top any more, but maybe one of your friends would look great in it. And you save money by not having to buy new clothes! Why not make it into a pamper party and spoil each other with some new hair looks?

For more ideas go to cathycassidy.com

How can you make your WISHES and DREAMS ❤ come TRUE? ❤

WISHES and DREAMS are just other words for positive thinking, and that's something that can be very powerful! Get together with friends and create some beautiful dream flags to start the magic . . .

You will need:

✦ A3 white or coloured paper

✦ Coloured crayons, felt pens, oil pastels, water-based paints, brushes, scissors, glue, glitter, sequins, yarn, foil streamers, tinsel, stickers, stars, tissue paper, ribbon, gold/silver pens, assorted collage materials

✦ A long length of string/coloured cord/ribbon

✦ IMAGINATION!!!

How to make your DREAM FLAG:

✦ Take your piece of A3 paper and cut it in half lengthways. Then fold each piece in half so you have two long thin strips of paper. This will give you 2 flags.

✦ Use paints, pens, crayons, pastels or a combination to pattern/colour the paper. Or collage your flag with ribbon, foil, stars and paper.

✦ Write your dream on to the flag shape. If you'd rather keep the dream secret, just decorate the flag with your own patterns and symbols, but think about your dream while you are doing this.

✦ Use both sides of the flag, or get your friend to use the other side so you can share the dream flag!

✦ Fold your flag over the string/cord and staple or glue your flag into place . . . then hang the dream flags along a wall or classroom!

Follow your dreams with all cathy cassidy's gorgeous books

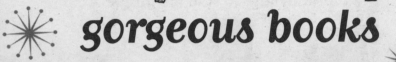

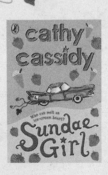

Brand new from cathy cassidy

Angel Cake

Anya used to dream of moving to Britain to start a brand-new life. But as she sits in a school where nobody understands her, she dreams of Polish summer skies and the place where she belonged.

Then Anya meets bad boy Dan. He's no angel, but she's sure there's a sweeter side to him. And when things fall apart at school, Anya realizes she's not alone - how can Dan be such bad news when being with him feels like heaven?

catch all of the latest news and gossip from

cathy cassidy

at

cathycassidy.com

sneaky peeks at new titles

details of signings and events near you

audio extracts and interviews with cathy

post your messages and pictures

Don't miss a word!

Sign up to receive a FREE email newsletter from Cathy into your Inbox every month

Go to cathycassidy.com